The Harmonics of Sound, Color and Vibration

*A System for
Self-Awareness
and Soul Evolution*

Elias DeMohan
(William David)

DEVORSS *Publications*

The Harmonics of Sound, Color & Vibration
Copyright © 1980
by W. William David Dumitru

ISBN: 0-87516-411-0
Library of Congress Catalog Card No. 80-65899
Sixth Printing, 2001

DeVorss & Company, Publisher
P.O. Box 550
Marina del Rey, CA 90294-0550

www.devorss.com

Printed in The United States of America

To The Esoteric Philosophy Center and the group of students who provided the opportunity to bring forth this system for sharing.

Elias DeMohan

ACKNOWLEDGMENTS

I would like to express my appreciation and gratitude to Luanna Anderson, Liane Crawford, Maynard Dalton, Wynelle Delaney, Dell Gibson, Jannah Gibson, Margaret Gibson, Susan Gough, Cynthia Jackson, Ewell Jackson, Hazel Kiley, Al Louvier, Ron Mercer, Mel Oliver, and Patricia Phillips for their time, dedication and assistance in assembling the material, writing and editing of this book. Also, I would like to thank Master D.K. for the assistance and encouragement in formulating this system.

I also want to especially acknowledge and thank Joan McSherry and Joe Rioux, co-founders of The Esoteric Philosophy Center, for their encouragement and support in sharing the vision and purpose of creating a school where systems such as this can be developed and shared for service.

TABLE OF CONTENTS

LIST OF FIGURES

LIST OF TABLES

FOREWORD

This book is designed to present mystical esoteric knowledge in a practical, workable system to enhance and accelerate the evolutionary process for a smoother transition into the new age, the Aquarian Age. The system presented has been brought through the consciousness of William David, guided and inspired from the Hierarchy by the Master consciousness, Djwhal Khul. Master D.K., or The Tibetan as he often calls himself, is one of the Masters responsible for setting up educational systems and was also the inspiration behind the writings of Alice A. Bailey.

William David is an accomplished Akashic reader and has helped many people to gain new understandings through the information he is able to give them on their past life experiences. He began giving readings in 1966, and through this sharing experience with others has learned much about the cosmic and human evolutionary process. The Akashic records are the records or memories of all time sometimes called "The Book of Life." Everything that has ever happened is duly recorded and available for Service to those who are aware. Our records or memories surround us in our energy fields, but until we gain enough awareness to be able to interpret them for ourselves, we may turn to those who can.

Among other experiences, William David's soul has specialized in akashic reading, having trained for thirteen lifetimes to gain the expertise manifested today in the personality of William David. It is as though our soul communicates to his soul the information that we need for more self-conscious awareness, and that information is then translated into language we can understand. This information must be requested by the personality and received with the sense of responsibility it entails. Awareness always brings responsibility.

1

Edgar Cayce, the famous psychic from Virginia Beach, often attributed his source of information to the akashic records. Although Cayce and many akashic readers work from a trance or unconscious state, William David has the capability to do readings with full conscious awareness.

In his youth, William David aspired to be an opera singer and spent years in voice training. This training in breathing and sound took him through many initiations into self-conscious awareness of his soul's purpose and service this lifetime. It prepared him for the teaching he would be doing in later years as he helps students gain awareness and balance with the use of diaphragmatic breathing, sound, color and vibration.

In 1960, as a student in a meditation class, William David was told by his teacher, from a trance state, that he would be teaching sound, color and vibration in the future. He was not even aware at that time of what this meant. He continued in this class and other studies until 1967 when he began to give serious thought to forming an esoteric school. As he began to accept the responsibilities of his soul's direction, he started to investigate the methods he should use in teaching. He was directed to read *Esoteric Psychology I* and *Esoteric Psychology II, Letters on Occult Meditation,* Chapter Seven, and *A Treatise on White Magic,* "Rule Four," all by Alice A. Bailey.

On further inquiry, he was aware of direct inner communication with Master D.K. and was advised to begin his instructions with what he knew about sound and breathing; for as he shared, more information would be given on the Eastern, Western and Oriental methods as well as the Tibetan schools of synthesis. He was admonished, however, that his teachings should be based upon his experiences and that theories or abstract concepts were to be identified as such.

Later direction came to begin a school in Houston, Texas,

and The Esoteric Philosophy Center, Inc., a non-profit
school of new age education, was founded in July, 1970.
The first classes in sound, color and vibration started in
October, 1970, and the system presented here began its evolutionary process through the next seven years.

The schools of the Aquarian Age will take another step in
the evolution of education by promoting group work, student participation and practice instead of just verbal and
mental communication of theories and abstract knowledge.
As the students experience this new process of education
and are willing to relate and share their experiences with
their group, they are provided supportive and sustaining
energy by the group while accelerating their evolutionary
process into more and more self-conscious awareness.

As the classes in sound, color and vibration expanded and
evolved for the next five years, plans were made to share the
process with others through a book. William David and a
few students devised an outline of what information should
be included. Later, another group of students and teachers
began weekly meetings to assemble the necessary information into workable units. It took another three years to attain the first draft, edit, assemble the illustrations and begin
to submit the manuscript for publication.

Although this may seem a slow process, it is a creditable
achievement when one realizes the group work that was accomplished as so many were willing to lend their time, talent
and cooperation on an extended basis to bring this project
to fruition. The writing of this book was not accomplished
through withdrawal into one-pointed concentration and
daily discipline, but was written in addition to the work,
teaching, study, and personal responsibilities of each group
member as time allowed. A triune of energies (the consciousness of Master D.K., William David, and the group of students and teachers) manifested this creative process into
form. The Aquarian Age will be the age of group work; the

willingness of the individual to blend his talents and expertise into one creative whole. The need for individual recognition will give way to group recognition through soul awareness which will guide mankind into the true understanding of brotherhood and service.

Many of those who have experienced group work will attest to the difficulties and stress one may experience in blending one's individual consciousness into a group consciousness. We are aware our efforts today are but a seed in light of the fruition to come into full expression later in the Aquarian Age. Still, we strive to accept ourselves and others as we seek to adopt a new point of view: *Sharing means twice as much; not half as much.*

This system is one of many for accelerating evolution and awareness. As we enter the changing of an age, the energies are necessarily amplified and the opportunity for individual acceleration is therefore available and encouraged. As with most spiritual and mystical information, we can offer no scientific proof except that many of us have experienced the process and find it valid. We encourage you to be open in evaluating for yourself the information presented and to trust your inner feeling. If there is a feeling of knowing . . . this could be so . . . ; begin the process and more understanding will come. If not, feel free to investigate other sources.

Those who know William David will agree he has a ready wit and incredible sense of humor. As you begin this process, we encourage you to develop and maintain your sense of humor for this is the most healing and balancing of all attributes.

Truth is ever expanding awareness. We do not espouse a philosophy of *one* truth, dogma or religion. If there is *one* truth, it is change and expansion of consciousness to greater and greater awareness which eventually makes previous truth obsolete. That is the cosmic process of enlightenment and service.

INTRODUCTION

The advent of the atomic era has had a sobering effect on mankind. A unique weapon has been developed which, if used indiscriminately, is sufficiently powerful to obliterate the surface of the Earth with the apparent obvious consequences. Of necessity, a profound change in socio-political thinking has occurred and a means of international cooperation is now deemed essential. Thus, the world's most powerful weapon has become a political instrument as we enter upon the threshold of a New Age, the Aquarian Age. The long-awaited age of brotherhood and cooperation is beginning with fear and respect for power instead of with understanding and trust.

Continuous improvement in communication media of all types—visual, audio and written—has made accessible a wide variety of information on previously censored subjects which stimulate self-awareness and self-acceptance. The vast information available on all subjects, including esoteric knowledge, has provided man with an enormous quantity of ideas.

In the past, educators have had to be discriminating in presenting esoteric teachings, as few were ready to understand the concepts. Prejudice and persecution of the teachers was not unusual; esoteric writings, as well as teachings, were necessarily veiled in symbology and analogy.

Past reticence was well-founded; and preservation, more than dissemination, of esoteric knowledge became the prime concern. Today, scientific discoveries and technologies have placed forces in the hands of mankind without the spiritual understanding imparted by esoteric knowledge. This alone may be reason enough to begin an orderly dispensing of the basic philosophy.

The beginning of the Age of Aquarius is bringing awareness for the need to cooperate, to recognize the value of shared knowledge, and to serve; it is the age of individualized consciousness within a group. The true meaning of Aquarian Age service is defined as a sharing of abundance, the result of one's overflowing, rather than a fulfilling of personal desires. One cannot force this service upon others or "will" it to happen. It is not sacrificial to the server and does not imply a debt to the recipient. One serves by *Beingness* rather than dutiful, willful giving.

There is an urgent need at this time for active cooperation and participation in the evolutionary plan. The Solar Logos and our entire solar system is experiencing a cyclic phase of tremendous expansion and growth. Thus, the planet Earth is also expanding its consciousness. As we endeavor to expand our own consciousness in preparation for the new age, we enhance the process on all other levels and, conversely, their expansion enhances ours. With the cooperation gained from this awareness, we can aid each other for a smoother transition by releasing our own resistances and actively seeking expansion.

Ancient wisdom teaches that all planets are soul-entities in the process of their own evolution as well as rendering service. The consciousness of the Earth is the mother consciousness, as she provides the necessary process for the development of the sons of God into enlightenment or creative Suns. As the Earth achieves its own enlightenment or full self-conscious awareness, we who dwell upon its physical and within its etheric body are necessarily a part of that process as Earth is a part of ours. The Earth has a nervous system, heart center, and other chakras as we do, and must be treated with the same care and consideration that we would want for our own physical form.

As we expand, the consciousness of Earth expands; and as the consciousness of Earth expands, we expand. We are, of necessity, closely cooperating cosmic partners in evolution. Let us respect our responsibility in this partnership with consciousness awareness. We must be aware of the effect our scientific and technological skills are having upon the soul-entity consciousness and form of Mother Earth as we invade her etheric body, her physical form, and even her innermost vital organs and nervous system. What far-reaching effects will this have on the weather, Earth changes, fuel resources, etc.? Are we achieving a balanced interchange for enlightenment, or heading for another cataclysm like Atlantis? Are we raping, without awareness, the planet that has mothered us? What will the consequences be to Earth and all mankind?

You ask, "What can I do?" Begin with yourself. Your individual expansion process is service while preparing you for greater service personally and as a group member. Knowledge and use of sound, color, and vibration, together with the breathing techniques, enhance and accelerate the process, thus serving the soul, the Earth and the entire solar system. Remember, you cannot give in service anything that you have not first received for yourself.

Discussion 1: Esoteric Philosophy

A Brief Definitive Overview of the
Eastern, Western, Oriental
and Tibetan Schools
Review of Esoteric Concepts
Vibration
Sound
Color (Table A)
Tantra
Reincarnation
Karma (Table B)
Time and Initiation—Systems for
Measuring Progress
Figure 1

A BRIEF DEFINITIVE OVERVIEW OF THE EASTERN, WESTERN, ORIENTAL AND TIBETAN SCHOOLS

The Eastern, Western, Oriental, and Tibetan philosophies, or schools, represent different concepts of vibrational energy patterns which must be experienced by the soul for the evolution of consciousness in Earth. Each school represents an intensity of development in a different area of consciousness which emphasizes one of the primary color qualities—red, blue, and yellow. While each philosophy embraces the other in many aspects, they are also constantly evolving and synthesizing on all levels with the concepts of the others. After the soul has experienced the polarity lessons of balancing energies in each school, and integrated them in consciousness through many lifetimes, a synthesizing process takes place bringing the necessary balance and flow for creative wholeness from the philosophy of the Tibetan schools.

For identification, the following descriptions will briefly characterize, as simply as possible, the evolutionary patterns represented by each school. Please note, these are short explanations describing the essence quality of each school and not its totality. Many excellent books have been written with indepth explanations if more information is desired.

The Western schools of Egypt, North Africa, Europe, North America and South America represent the color red and emphasize the development of the physical body through feeling and action. Here consciousness identifies with the physical form and learns to sustain and operate it for peak performance. This evolves a sense of self-reliance through physical power. Two of the high points in the history of the Western schools were the Greek olympias and the Greek sculptures exemplified by the temples of Diana, Aphrodite and Apollo, which were dedicated to the appreciation of the body beautiful and its capabilities of action and reaction to movement developed through sports and hygiene.

The Western concepts embrace individual independence in operating the physical sensual (feeling) nature through intelligent activity with awareness. These schools also emphasize materiality and the importance of creating form for enjoyment as seen in Western society today. They develop the qualities of will and power expressed through action, vocal sound and rhythm. This school has developed the broad use of the vowel sound in opera and blended the sounds of instruments in symphonies. In extreme, this consciousness can be aggressive, causing war and strife.

The Eastern schools of India and the lands of Hindustan represent the color blue and emphasize emotional development through idealism, mysticism, and spiritual aspiration, as they seek to transcend the physical into other dimensions of awareness. They often express idealistic devotion to love relationships, to their teachers, gurus and to God. Through meditation and physical discipline, they seek to overcome the physical and material world, which they consider illusionary. They are determined to accept the will of God as true reality and thus attain a state of oneness with the Creator, or Nirvana. Through melodious movement, color, instrumental music, mantras and mandalas, they espouse the qualities of compassion, kindness and gentleness with acceptance.

The Eastern schools seek and depend upon answers from outside of themselves through spiritual quest. In return, they give themselves with devotion to their ideals, evolving the qualities of faith through reflection and receptivity. The study of philosophy and theology and the development of idealism are their primary concerns. The female is highly revered in their spiritual concepts. In extreme, this consciousness can be very secretive, devious and possessive.

The Oriental schools of China and Japan represent the color yellow. They value mental skills, which they use to control and direct the physical and feeling-emotional departments into harmonious relationship. The body becomes a precise instrument of the mind for experiencing, as mental evaluations of judgment and criticism control the feelings and emotions. They know how to use sound vibrations to create thoughtforms into manifestation. Seeking to create perfection through mental precision, they develop a scientific analytical approach to experiencing life, eventually evolving the yellow quality of discrimination (joy through understanding).

The Oriental schools teach traditions, such as ancestor worship, which create a sense of authority and security through continuity, developing the ability to organize and administrate patterns of relationships for efficiency. Through these mental processes eventually evolves the consciousness of detached involvement, an awareness of immortality, and an ability to bring spiritual ideals into manifest reality.

Sounds in the Oriental schools are very precise and mental, with little feeling or emotion, and can be hypnotic in effect. Thus, they traditionally do not applaud to show feelings of approval and enjoyment after a theatrical performance. The martial arts of Kung Fu, Karate, Zen and gymnastics are examples of the Oriental schools and exemplify how they can use movement and sound to defeat their opponents; they disrupt the stability of the opponent's emotional body by the release of power through sound. In extreme, this consciousness can be too traditional, judgmental, critical, manipulative and calculating.

This school will be more prominent in development as we proceed into the Aquarian Age and humanity as a whole enters into a period of intense mental evolution. This is already being seen in the popularity of the martial arts, especially gymnastics and the new expansion of China into the affairs of the planet.

The Tibetan schools of Tibet, Afghanistan, and part of Central Asia use sound, color and vibration to harmonize the physical, feeling-emotional, and mental departments for synthesis into an intuitional creative Being. They are able to be very flowing, to extend to other dimensions with awareness, and to be highly creative through these abilities. They represent the color indigo, and are tantric in expression as they relate to energy force-fields. Their sounds are futuristic, and bells are often used for their quality of resonance is representative of synthesis. They develop the consciousness of service through Being. In extreme, they can be very isolated; but remember, all extremes are necessary to each school for a time until a balance and flow in consciousness can be established through experience for properly relating the concepts.

The schools become prominent at certain periods in history according to the evolutionary need of the planet and humanity. These cyclical periods of an overall emphasis into one of the energy streams can be seen throughout an Age. Yet, within that major cycle there are many minor cycles, even as few as ten or twelve years, when there is an alternating emphasis on one of the other schools for balance.

The Piscean Age has been primarily under the direction of the Western schools, whose responsibility it has been to combine the Eastern philosophies with the Western. For example, the Western concepts of freedom and independence are being developed on some levels through the Eastern concepts of dependence upon religious or spiritual guidance. In order to effect this, mini-cycles alternately directed by one of the schools create an emphasis upon certain concepts which are then blended into a newer concept or creative whole.

In every culture in the world today, there can be found all four schools interrelating within an overall dominance of one school. There are also many evolutionary levels of consciousness within each culture and school, expressing according to their experience and understanding, which can be quite diversified.

It is very important to understand that this is also the evolutionary pattern of individual soul consciousness. Therefore, there is constant interrelating of these energy streams within the individual consciousness as they are experienced. A soul-entity consciousness may be experiencing an emphasis in development withone one or another school cyclically throughout a lifetime, but because of the interrelating, there will not be as distinct a separation as the previous descriptions in this overview. One must look for the overall concepts to identify a predominant school.

A REVIEW OF ESOTERIC CONCEPTS

VIBRATION

Vibration is the name given to the cyclic wave length frequencies of energy force-fields. It is the rhythm or primary oscillatory movement of any animate or inanimate object. Generally, on Earth's three-dimensional plane, vibration is manifested as sound, color, light and form.

Melody is that inner awareness of sound that has, through accepting experiencing, evolved from noise to a melodic vibration that experiences feelings with movement or emotion. In a sense, it combines sound and color within the individual.

Color harmony manifests as synthesis of rhythm and melody in the energy bodies of the human form. The physical, feeling-emotional and mental bodies of the entity have become balanced and are able to brilliantly radiate the resulting auric field that is seen, felt or heard by those with psychic capability.

Every element in the universe has an energy force-field, as basic vibrational rhythm, and possesses the capability of increasing and directing the frequency of that vibrational rhythm. As consciousness becomes sufficiently self-consciousness aware, its vibrational rate is increased to the point of light, for example, the Sun.

All elements with a minimum of conscious awareness, not to be confused with self-conscious awareness, have a certain capacity to interact with other elements, which creates a spiraling effect. The more the element experiences interaction with other elements, the more conscious awareness it develops. This leads to a higher individual vibrational frequency, enabling the element to interact with greater facility. This interaction leads to additional experiencing with increased awareness and so on in an ever-expanding spiral.

In Earth's three-dimensional plane, the mineral kingdom has the slowest vibrational frequency. Few minerals are capable of interaction with the human kingdom; however, those that do interact, do so primarily through their color and have become known as precious and semi-precious gems. Their interaction can sometimes be felt as heat or a similar type of energy manifestation to the aware human. These precious or semi-precious gems, interacting through color, have a healing quotient for the human kingdom. The healing powers of various minerals were historically well-known and probably one of the main reasons humans collected them and made them precious. Gold, silver and some other metals fall into the same category.

The purest mineral stones have higher vibrations; diamonds have the highest. Healing qualities of minerals have been greatly enhanced by man's cutting and polishing of them, helping to reflect their color qualities with much greater intensity.

Interestingly, some semi-precious stones are vibrationally more in tune with the general human populace than the precious ones and can be more readily utilized for healing by most people. The vibrational rate of a good malachite stone can be felt by many people. Amber, petrified pine resin, is another stone with renowned healing properties.

The next level of conscious awareness, or vibrational level of Earth, is the plant kingdom. Sufficient experiments have been performed to prove that plants have response-awareness and do interact with other consciousnesses. The book, *The Secret Life of Plants,* by Peter Tompkins and Christopher Bird, is an excellent source of information about this interaction.

Just as with the mineral kingdom, the plant kingdom has a hierarchy of vibrational frequency levels. The highest level plants are those with fragrant blossoms and fruit, closely followed by cereal grains. The healing qualities of well-known plants and herbs reflect similar vibrations.

Hallucinogenic plants such as marijuana, mushrooms, peyote and poppies have been used esoterically for various purposes throughout history. Of course, this use was mostly done under supervision and for a specific purpose. Since these hallucinogens primarily affect the etheric and astral bodies, the individual's conscious awareness of the altered states is limited. Sound, color, movement and meditation can provide effective alternatives for affecting the etheric and astral bodies, allowing the student to experience deeper and more controlled states of altered consciousness with awareness.

The animal kingdom is the third level of vibrational frequency on Earth. Animals have a sensory conscious awareness of other vibrational energy fields and use sound and body movement for communication. They primarily follow genetic, cyclic, instinctual and sensual patterns of reactive behavior to stimuli and do not create new patterns of behavior at a self-conscious level.

The human kingdom is the fourth vibrational frequency level on Earth. Here begins self-conscious awareness accompanied by the realization that one's own energy force-field vibration has an ever-increasing effect on surrounding force-fields and those fields of energy have a reciprocal effect on one's own force-field. There is an ongoing interrelatedness and interchange between heightened vibrational frequencies and self-conscious awareness. This stimulates an accompanying awareness of the multi-dimensional aspects of human existence and the necessity for accepting responsibility for one's own actions and reactions. A more detailed discussion of man's evolution through vibrational levels of the human kingdom is included later in "Discussion 1" under Reincarnation. Vibration, sound, color and movement have been utilized throughout the ages to assist the human kingdom in achieving greater self-conscious awareness.

SOUND

Sound is the result of interactions between frequency vibrations of energy force-fields. The lower frequency levels are either unheard or manifested as noise. As vibrational levels increase, noise becomes sound; as sound is more refined, it becomes music. This is a result of resistances between levels of vibrational frequencies.

In its earliest use, sound with awareness was for communication. As practitioners of sound became more proficient, consonants and vowels were developed. Consonants are utilized for inner self-awareness. The "hum" ("m" and "n" sounds) gives the highest point of inner awareness and brings flow to inner blockages. The "hum" may be used to center our force-field, preventing unwanted intrusion from outer forces.

Vowels are utilized to facilitate outer awareness and outer relationships. Vowel sounds are required to reach other vibrational force-fields for relating. By combining consonants with vowels, sound is projected for more effective communication.

As the use of sound became more proficient, humans discovered that it could raise their vibrational levels. The combined use of sound and color stimulated memory for greater self-conscious awareness. Vowel sounds, in particular, were held sacred by rulers in various schools of esoteric knowledge. At times, vowel sounds were used by the rulers to maintain control, or sometimes these sounds were withheld from the masses because people were insufficiently experienced to be capable of utilizing them effectively.

Today, knowledge concerning the utilization of sound is available and open to those who seek it out and are willing to practice its manifestation. Sound is an important tool for increasing vibrational frequency and expanding self-conscious awareness.

COLOR

Color is another manifestation of vibration and stimulates sensitivity through the human form. Its associated qualities are shown in Table A. One characteristic of color is its ability to create a response without conscious awareness. As color is perceived and transmitted to the brain, the mind is activated to create imagery and more color. This is analogous with the explanation of vibrational frequency fields, in that color activates a spiraling effect or progressive movement in consciousness.

Color hues can be perceived only with sufficient experience through memories. As colors and their associated

TABLE A
THE RAYS AND THEIR COLOR QUALITIES

RAY	COLOR	SOUND	HARMONIOUS QUALITIES	RESISTANT QUALITIES
I	Red	Ē (Be)	Freedom, determination, honor, will, power, strength, activity, pioneer, alertness, independence, feeling, inspiration, motivation, rhythm, spontaneity, initiative, leadership.	Anger, authoritarianism, lust, frustration, force, confusion, violence, destruction, revenge, rebellion, impulsive, impatient, vengeance
II	Blue	Ō (No)	Love, wisdom, gentleness, trust, understanding, detachment, kindness, compassion, patience, forgiveness, cooperation, melody, sensitivity, contemplation, emotional	Possessiveness, self-pity, fear, self-rejection, indifference, separateness, isolation, worry, depression, passive, anxiety, coldness, detachment
III	Yellow	Ä (Ah)	Joy, expression, ability, mental discrimination, organization, attention to detail, evaluation, active intelligence, discipline, administration, praise, sincerity, harmony	Criticism, crystallization, lazy, over-indulgence, stubborn, constriction, contempt, sorrow, selfish, cowardice, judgmental, bitterness, cynical, agnostic

			Positive qualities	Negative qualities
IV	Green	Ā (Hay)	All of the qualities of yellow and blue exist in green plus: enthusiasm, responsiveness, acceptance, hope, sharing, sustenance, expansion, growth, symphony	All of the qualities of yellow and blue above plus: jealousy, envy, regimentation, stinginess, pessimism, disorder, resistance, greed, vindictive
V	Orange	Ě (Bet)	All of the above qualities of red and yellow plus: illumination, courage, analysis, steadfastness, victory, confidence, intellect, change, striving, inventive, assertive, self-motivation	All of the qualities of red and yellow above plus: uncooperative, sluggish, ignorance, inferiority, superiority, cruelty, pompous, procrastination, aggressive
VI	Purple-Violet	Ü (You)	All of the qualities of red and blue above plus: mercy, devotion, responsibility, loyalty, understanding of justice, idealism, meditative, reflective, wisdom, grace	All the qualities of red and blue above plus: obsession, injustice, martyrdom, restriction, morose, intolerant, agitation, impotence, retribution, punishment
VII	Indigo	ŌM (Home)	Synthesis, inspirational, ritual, ceremonial magic, implementation, catalyst, aspiration, unity, calm, balance, world service, humanitarian	Pride, separateness, conceit, arrogance, contempt, resentment, totalitarianism, irritability, gossip, deceit, rigidity

qualities are perceived and experienced, one's vibrational frequency is increased, which allows more and purer color qualities to be discerned, manifested and experienced. This increases the vibrational frequency, again allowing purer color qualities to be experienced. Finally, colors and their qualities are comprehended, experienced and manifested as pure white light, when the entity is said to be "Christed."

Color is manifested in the auric field by expanding the vibrational frequency of the spiral. As the auric field becomes increasingly pure in color, it eventually becomes white light which has an extended effect on the immediate environment. One's vibrational frequency acts with greater intensity on nearby energy fields and stimulates additional activity and heightened awareness. Through this intensified vibrational frequency, the entity serves others and motivates his own self-conscious awareness simply by Being.

TANTRA

Tantra, or Tantric Yoga, as it has become known, is basically a catch-all term that has been given to a school of sound and color. It evolved from Lemuria through Atlantis and Tibet into a school of philosophy that combined the use of vibration, sound and color, with movement, dance, rhythm and fragrance. The general purpose of this philosophy was to master the body's density. Body movement with feeling and mental awareness allowed the flow of soul energy to permeate the form. Tantra became a school for awareness using techniques for balancing the physical, feeling-emotional and mental bodies through knowledge and use of creative sound-movement energies.

Understanding the chakras started with Tantra, and through this, came awareness of the male-female principle of opposite polarities. Sex and orgasms were utilized to awaken the kundalini, using that primal energy to open chakras for awareness. The physical orgasm achieved through sex or body movement was the first and earliest awareness of the sensitivity of the soul. The major intensity of the physical orgasm is centered in the senses. Later, feeling-emotional orgasms through the creative arts such as music, painting and sculpture opened further pathways to the soul; the major intensity here was centered in color. The mental orgasm comes through the inventive arts such as architecture, mathematics or philosophy with the intensity centered in mental awareness. Tantra, in its purest essence, attempts to balance these and provide a joy of living through relating to others along with an acceptance and love of self and all of creation.

REINCARNATION—An Evolutionary Plan for Expansion

Alice A. Bailey, in *A Treatise on White Magic,* states that all that is, is the result of a life force expressing in the manifested universe. Thus one central universal energy pervades all forms and produces universal consciousness. She explains that the unfoldment of this universal consciousness is the purpose of all manifestation or life forms. This unfoldment occurs by evolution, shaping matter into form within the space-time continuum.

The shaping of matter into form compresses the original life force energy into simple atoms, then atoms of greater complexity, further into molecules, further yet into compounds, minerals, stones and eventually into the planets as the Earth. This tendency toward compression leads to more complex matter arrangements, which in turn leads to higher levels of consciousness within these forms. Finally, at the level of the nucleoprotein cell, conscious awareness begins.

Universal consciousness has made a great leap forward. Enclosed in a membrane, it manifests as an inside and an outside, a self and not-self, the point within the circle. The primal drive toward more intricate forms of matter and amplification of consciousness continues as evolutionary processes expand toward increasingly complex life forms. Consciousness continues to evolve through these life forms until it becomes a brain. This brain matter becomes more complex, and consciousness amplifies until homosapien, "the one who knows," evolves. Physical evolution then gives way to the evolution of ideas in the realm of pure mind. Universal consciousness unfolds to produce individualized consciousness.

The basic underlying element in this evolutionary process of expanding consciousness is experiencing. This experiencing, with evaluation and acceptance, brings expansion and is true of all levels of life, from the most infinitesimal to man, the solar system, and ultimately the universal source, God. The three-dimensional Earth plane, in which humanity presently finds itself, is only one step in this infinite plan of expansion. It is a step that is taken by choice. In general, humans will pass through seven levels of consciousness in the Earth's plane. Table B shows these stages of experiential development.

The primitive or seed soul-entity of tribal consciousness is ruled by fear, senses and instinct. Unknown forces govern actions and beliefs; functioning is on a physical survival level. The tribal peer group progresses by experiencing, and eventually the mass consciousness level, governed by taboos, evolves.

The mass consciousness soul-entity progresses from purely physical fear of the unknown to a more feeling-emotional fear of breaking the rules of the peer group. The leaders of this group establish rules which become traditions. This experiencing enables the soul-entity to enter the individual consciousness level, the beginning of self awareness.

The individual level accepts a concept of good and evil

which becomes the governing factor. The leaders, either political, religious, or both, establish the precepts of what is good for the group and the individual or what acts are considered evil for the group and its participants. The soul-entity can experience actions considered as "good" and receive wide acclaim; actions considered "evil" will be punished by political or religious lawmakers and peers. Eventually, the soul-entity expands to the point where the mores and rules of the group are questioned and it begins to seek answers from self, thus entering into the aspirant level of consciousness.

The aspirant begins to explore his concepts of life and no longer accepts the group's concepts of good and evil. Here begins the field of science, intellect, and facts that are proven by constant repetitive evaluations. In the beginning, there is a dependency upon teachers, gurus and religious organizations. Later may follow a time of cynicism, agnosticism and atheism, until finally responsibility is accepted for individual thoughts and actions. Now begins an active search for the understanding of self and self's relationship with the universe. No longer one of the peer group, the aspirant further individualizes through experiencing and studying. Self-knowledge is realized and progression to the disciple level of consciousness is attained.

At the disciple level of consciousness, rules of political or religious leaders no longer bind the entity, as experience teaches right action, regardless of what the majority of people consider right or wrong. The assumption of responsibility for one's own actions eliminates the individual's need for laws which prevent people from harming each other. Experiencing—including studying and learning about one's self—paves the way to the initiate level of consciousness.

The initiate begins the experiencing of serving the master plan for Earth. Gaining knowledge and understanding of one's self brings about a vibrational level which serves by

TABLE B
LEVELS OF CONSCIOUSNESS

PLANES	CONSCIOUSNESS LEVEL	AWARENESS	DISTINGUISHING CHARACTERISTICS
7 (49)*	MASTER-SOUL	HIERARCHY	Soul-entity completes Earth plane experiences and chooses to serve in Earth's plane or move on to other planes.
6 (49)*	INITIATE	SERVICE	Knows and understands harmlessness; serves by Being. Group service.
5 (49)*	DISCIPLE	SELF-KNOWLEDGE	Begins to know, think and experience for self. Effort toward group world service. Intuitive response.
4 (49)*	ASPIRANT	SEEKING or AGNOSTIC	Questions beliefs of peer group; begins to seek own answers. Intellectual and fact finding endeavors. Independence begins.

3 (49)*	INDIVIDUAL	GOOD and EVIL	Actions of individual considered by peer group as good or evil and rewarded or punished. Beginning of self-conscious awareness. Traditions—self-denial—duty—obedience.
2 (49)*	MASS	TABOOS	Unquestioning obedience to peer group's mores. Total dependency on authority; anthropomorphic beliefs.
1 (49)*	TRIBAL	PHYSICAL SURVIVAL	Fear and instinct rules actions; animalistic beliefs. Group survival and dependency.

* 49 sub-planes in each plane

simply Being. In experiencing the essence of various qualities, the individual becomes those qualities and cannot act otherwise. After a period of service and additional experiencing, expansion will proceed to the master soul level of consciousness.

The master soul level of consciousness serves the Hierarchy, those souls which work and guide with universal awareness. The soul-entity may elect to return to the Earth plane to serve the plan by specific action. Buddha, Jesus, and Mohammed achieved and demonstrated this level. The soul-entity may elect not to return to Earth's plane but serve at the Hierarchial level of existence, or progress to other planes to experience further or serve elsewhere.

The process of experiencing in the Earth plane is through reincarnation. This may be defined as cyclic rebirth into physical form. For most soul-entities, this process requires many lifetimes to evolve from the primitive tribal-mass consciousness to the position of a truly self-conscious aware individual capable of standing alone with clear, accurate and creative faculty of thought. During this process, a soul-entity may move through several minor-key lifetimes, doing small tasks, making minor advancements, in general preparing for a major-key lifetime. This major-key lifetime will bring increased interaction with others, complete many uncompleted experiences and make a giant step on the evolutionary journey. It may be chaotic and painful as resistances are met and experienced for greater awareness and acceptance, but it seems to be necessary for initiation to the higher planes of consciousness.

The experiencing process of reincarnation is necessary because no single lifetime would be sufficient to experience, accept, and synthesize all that is necessary for individual growth. Reincarnation serves as the means by which the soul-entity becomes a creative Sun or son of God. There is progressive experiencing of the seven levels of consciousness, producing increased self-conscious awareness. The experiences of incarnations eventually create greater dimensions of consciousness, with each incarnation contributing necessary experiences even though they may seem harmful or imbalanced. Extreme experiences are required in order that the individual learn and achieve the required balance for progressing to the next level of consciousness.

This evolutionary experiencing process is one of cause and effect; that is, the causes initiated in other lifetimes by different personalities, and not completed, must now be resolved as effects in this lifetime by this personality. In *A Treatise on White Magic*, Alice A. Bailey states that soul-entities on the mass-consciousness level, being swayed by mass ideas, and largely influenced by tradition and public opinion, do not direct their own development. The interaction of their lives causes certain predispositions for the future, but they are moved forward by the evolutionary process as it expresses through existing conditions. For the soul-entity who has attained a degree of self-conscious awareness, however, manifestation of the principle of cause and effect is based on individual thought and action. It is at this point in the evolution of the soul that planning is involved for unfoldment of subsequent life cycles.

KARMA—An Aid in Gaining Balance

This Earth plane system is one of opposites or polarities: good-evil, love-hate, success-failure, pride-humility, courage-fear, etc. As we experience the various physical, feeling-emotional and mental qualities of life, we often go to extremes which result in imbalance of a particular quality. Depending upon the magnitude of the imbalance, it may take several lifetimes experiencing with proper evaluation and understanding for the soul-entity to bring this quality back into harmony or balance. This is the law of karma in action. We all too often equate karmic law with retribution and punishment—something cruel and evil. In reality, it is simply experiencing that which is required in order to bring a particular quality aspect of life into balance. Karma may seem quite severe in those cases where corrective action meets an unusually high degree of resistance to change. It should be noted that we are also subject to other levels of karmic law such as race karma, human kingdom karma, planetary karma and solar system karma over which the individual has no direct control or awareness.

A SELF-IMPOSED PLAN FOR EXPERIENCING

A soul-entity starts existence as an individualized life force and must experience all the qualities in different dimensions for expansion to gain self-conscious awareness. Incarnation in the Earth's plane creates unbalanced actions because of the difficulty of experiencing within this slower vibrational field. Progressing from incarnation to incarnation, the soul-entity experiences and accepts the mean between the extremes, becoming a balanced, flowing, self-conscious aware individualized soul.

At completion of each incarnation, with the shedding of the conscious or concrete mind, an entity's soul consciousness takes stock of completed and incompleted actions. Figure 1 illustrates some of the qualities encountered through progressive incarnations for balance. As the soul progresses through a living personality, its completed actions expand and become a part of the basic soul energy field. Its incompleted or unaccepted actions manifest as "guilt" in the subconscious and are carried into subsequent incarnations for additional experiencing to achieve balance and harmony through acceptance.

Actions completed during incarnations increase soul consciousness and assist the entity in balancing incompleted actions in subsequent incarnations. At the completion of each incarnation, the soul evaluates the progress made to determine the quality of future experiencing. Although some experiencing is accomplished between incarnations, the three-dimensional physical plane appears to decrease the time required and expedites evolutionary progress. Once having reached the point of self-conscious awareness, the soul-entity plans the experiences needed for expansion in a subsequent lifetime.

This is not to say that all events are predestined; the entity always has the option to accept or reject experiences. Generally, the experiences that one encounters are chosen as necessary for growth and need to be accepted by the personality, regardless of society's response. Rejection only postpones the experience until a later time, while creating greater resistances to be worked through for acceptance.

Thus, the vibrational environment surrounding major events for experiences and decision making in life are of the soul's choosing. OUR LIFE IS WHAT OUR SOUL-ENTITY—SOUL AND PERSONALITY—PLANNED; NOT THE RESULT OF SOME RANDOM QUIRK OF FATE. WE MUST ACCEPT RESPONSIBILITY FOR OUR OWN LIFE AND CHOICES.

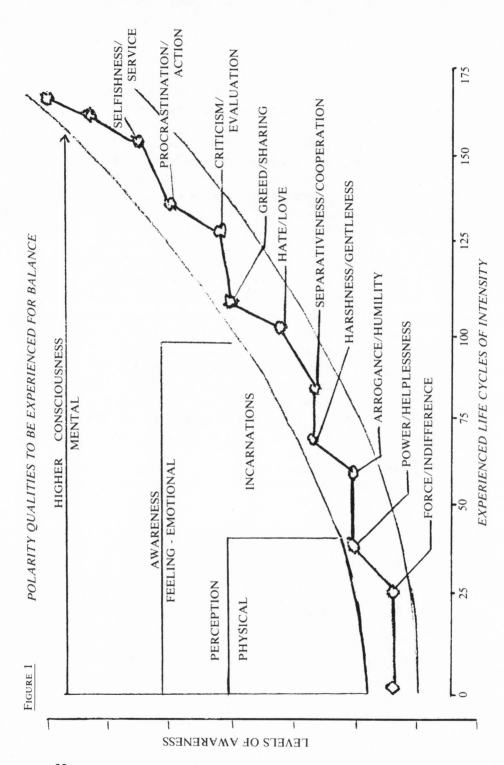

FIGURE 1

POLARITY QUALITIES TO BE EXPERIENCED FOR BALANCE

HIGHER CONSCIOUSNESS
MENTAL

AWARENESS
FEELING - EMOTIONAL

INCARNATIONS

PERCEPTION
PHYSICAL

SELFISHNESS/
SERVICE

PROCRASTINATION/
ACTION

CRITICISM/
EVALUATION

GREED/SHARING

HATE/LOVE

SEPARATIVENESS/COOPERATION

HARSHNESS/GENTLENESS

ARROGANCE/HUMILITY

POWER/HELPLESSNESS

FORCE/INDIFFERENCE

EXPERIENCED LIFE CYCLES OF INTENSITY

0   25   50   75   100   125   150   175

LEVELS OF AWARENESS

32

TIME AND INITIATION—SYSTEMS FOR MEASURING PROGRESS

Once an individual embarks upon a path of esoteric knowledge, the phenomenon of time must be viewed in a different context. The customary concepts of our time dimension may vary drastically from other possible dimensions and systems. In other systems or levels of consciousness, time may have a flexible nature and may expand or contract at the desire of the entity. Similarly, time may not have a serial characteristic; the past, present, and future may coincide. Such concepts of time are difficult, if not impossible, to visualize within our limited reference system. In the Earth plane, time is a most useful method of accountability and provides an excellent measure of one's evolutionary progress. Time may be used as a basis for determining an individual's record of past accomplishments and failures, as well as, a reference for providing focus on those experiences yet to be completed.

Figure 1 is an example of the polarities of experiences during incarnations. Acceptance in experiencing the polarities of life qualities increases self-conscious awareness and eventually achieves balance and flow for soul expansion.

For those who have achieved self-conscious awareness, an Initiation marks a point of attainment in expansion of consciousness. It signals entrance into a higher level of awareness along with a radical internal change of life perception with attendant responsibility. Initiation comes to all of us after the experiences of many lifetimes as we accept the life qualities. These acceptances arm us with the self-reliance and personality integration necessary for Initiation.

Each subsequent Initiation marks the passing of the soul-entity into an ever-increasing consciousness of cooperation with a growing capacity to perceive on all planes. Initiation

33

increases conscious awareness of the Universal Plan and the capability to serve the Plan.

When a soul-entity reaches the conclusion of its chosen life cycle on Earth and has experienced and properly evaluated all that it chose to achieve; when it has reached a point in consciousness where it is no longer held by the restraining forces of gravity and has become a creative, radiant, motivating point of Light or Sun of God; then it is ready to leave this Earth plane and move to another level of consciousness and experiencing.

Discussion 2: Personal Universe

THE PERSONAL UNIVERSE CONCEPT— THE PLAN

Each entity is a small personal universe consisting of matter, energy and consciousness. This personal universe is continuously striving to expand. It consists of radiant bodies within an auric space that is encompassed by the soul and is analogous to the astronomical planetary system which surrounds us. The radiant bodies will be described in detail in the following portions of this text. The complexity of the personal universe has confounded most clerics and scholars for aeons. In each age, however, there have been those few individuals with exceptional intuitive sensitivity who have led in analysis and definition of this concept. Even these gifted sensitives have had difficulties in translating their intuitional impressions into clear verbal description or illustrative graphics. Figures 2 and 3 present an attempt to graphically represent the personal universe concept, as the figures indicate the important elements in each personal universe, their general relationships, and the functions of each.

Figure 2 illustrates a concept of the auric space, the vibrational emanation characterized by sound and color qualities. The auric boundary of any unit cell entity will differ in size and shape depending upon its evolutionary status; similarly, there will be a variation in color and color intensity. Stored within the auric space are those incompleted experiences for which opportunities for completion are available during a given incarnation. These incompleted and unaccepted experiences of past life personalities comprise the subconscious. Also, encompassed within the auric space are completed experiences which can be utilized to facilitate balancing of incompleted actions. The incompleted actions may seem remote, dissimilar and disassociated with the soul-entity's present consciousness, but their completion, integration and subsequent utilization is required for a balanced expansion and a dedicated effort to open a communicative channel to higher levels of consciousness,

The personal universe is illustrated in Figure 3 with the elements discussed in Figure 2 repeated and shown to be a portion of the soul. The auric space provides the focus of energies during any given incarnation and contains all the capabilities, talents and qualities needed to successfully accomplish goals established for that lifetime. The soul also acts as a storehouse of the entity's completed experiences and plans for participation and expansion in the greater universal plan. It provides guidance to the entity during and between incarnations. A vast capability and consciousness is available to the entity when contact is made with the storehouse of the soul through the intuition.

The concepts illustrated in Figures 2 and 3 are simply pictorial representations of the principles involved. The relative sizes of the elements and boundaries are intended to show examples of differences in magnitudes of energies or intensities, and no specific application to a given individual is intended. These representations are offered to establish a reference which will be used throughout this text.

FIGURE 2

A CONCEPT OF AURIC SPACE
(Unit Cell of Energy Life)

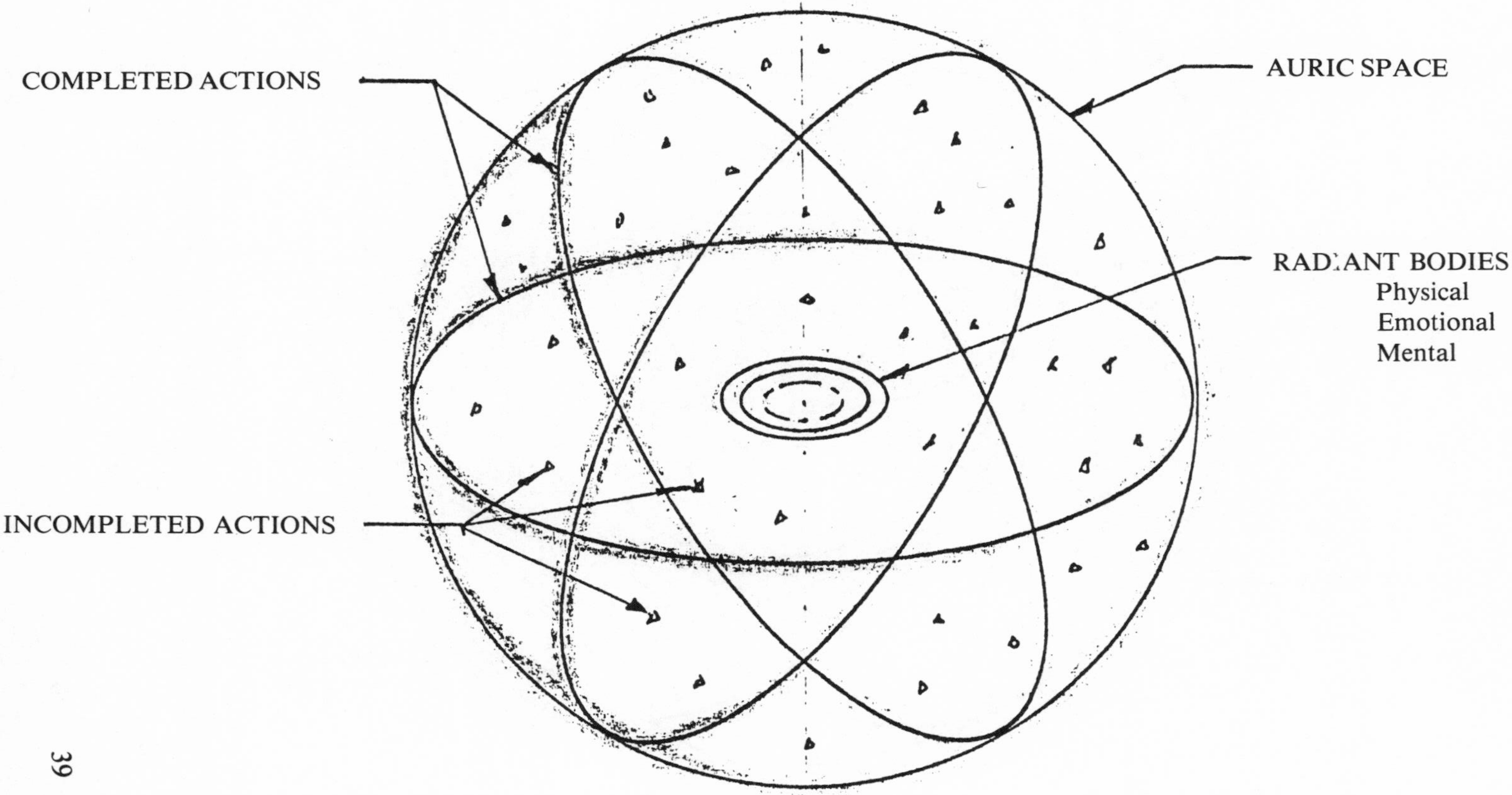

AURIC SPACE

RADIANT BODIES
Physical
Emotional
Mental

COMPLETED ACTIONS

INCOMPLETED ACTIONS

39

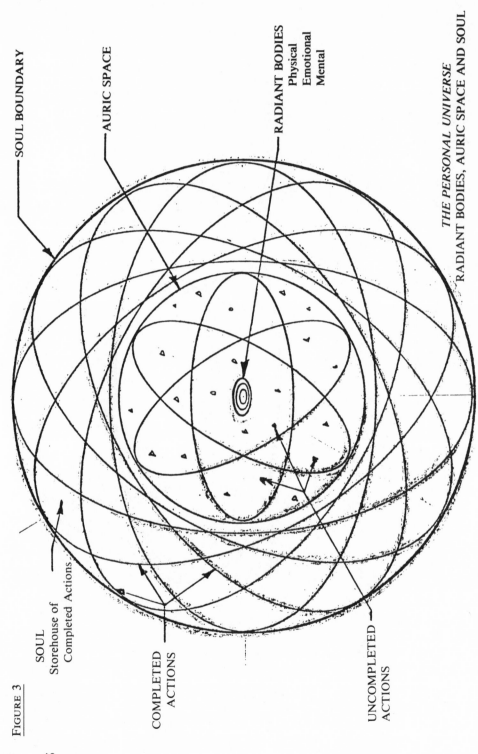

FIGURE 3

SOUL
Storehouse of
Completed Actions

SOUL BOUNDARY

AURIC SPACE

RADIANT BODIES
Physical
Emotional
Mental

COMPLETED
ACTIONS

UNCOMPLETED
ACTIONS

THE PERSONAL UNIVERSE
RADIANT BODIES, AURIC SPACE AND SOUL

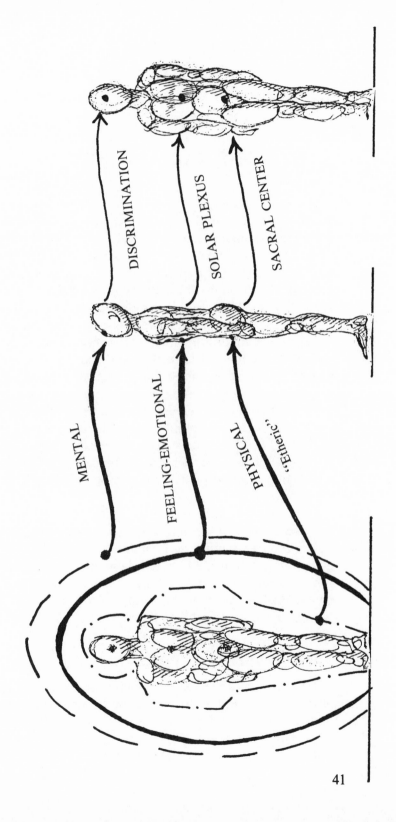

RADIANT BODIES AND CORRESPONDING CENTERS

MENTAL

FEELING-EMOTIONAL

PHYSICAL

"Etheric"

DISCRIMINATION

SOLAR PLEXUS

SACRAL CENTER

FIGURE 4

41

THE RADIANT BODIES

Discussion 1 indicated that consciousness takes form for the purpose of unfoldment and expansion through experiencing in this solar system. Figure 4 is a pictorial example of an entity's manifested form. Viewed collectively, the radiant bodies represent that element of consciousness, the entity or personality, through which the soul expresses itself on the Earth plane. The areas surrounding the physical form, referred to as the physical, feeling-emotional and mental bodies, are actually force fields of energy called the radiant bodies. These force fields reflect those basic qualities of life which must be experienced during various incarnations for expansion of a soul-entity's self-conscious awareness. Locations of the energy centers or chakras within the physical form which correspond to the radiant bodies are shown in Figure 4. The centers serve as focal points for these energy fields, and proper functioning of these body centers is important for advancement of an entity's level of consciousness.

Each of the radiant bodies manifests itself through definite recognizable characteristics dealing with qualities rather than masculine or feminine roles. There is an ongoing interrelationship between these qualities regardless of sex polarities in each lifetime. Figure 5 outlines these characteristics in summary form and the following paragraphs give a more detailed description.

RADIANT PHYSICAL BODY—ETHERIC BODY

The physical form is the manifestation of the etheric physical body and is the response apparatus for various parts of the personality. It manifests itself primarily through the feeling nature, the five senses of sight, smell, hearing, taste and touch. This physical form deals totally in a three-

42

THE RADIANT BODIES

PHYSICAL BODY (Etheric) - has qualities of responsiveness and performance. Uses instinct and all of the five senses: sight, smell, hearing, taste and touch. Employs perception and interaction.

FEELING-EMOTIONAL BODY - has qualities of the desire nature such as: love, hate, assurance, doubt, courage, fear and compassion. Has awareness through feelings, relationships, and color movement.

MENTAL BODY - is the essence of active intelligence. Has qualities such as: rules, regulations, evaluation, discipline, control and judgment. Has conscious awareness through discrimination and evaluation.

FIGURE 5

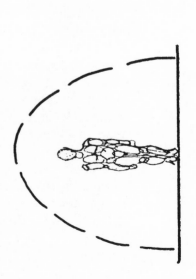
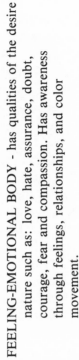
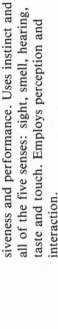

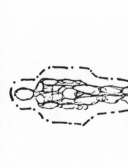

dimensional reality, with or without self-conscious awareness, depending upon the soul-entity's evolutionary level of
development. It is the mechanism through which a thought
from the mental body or a desire from the feeling-emotional
body is brought into form for experiencing as well as the instinctual mechanism of the five senses to outer stimuli which
leads to experiencing awareness and discrimination of the
physical environment.

The dense physical form is encased and permeated by a
web of energy currents called the etheric body. This web of
energy currents is the source through which the dense
physical form is energized and also forms the structure upon
which it manifests. Usually below the threshold of conscious
awareness, energy flow within the etheric body is generally
experienced in terms of vitality or lack of it. An important
thing to note about the etheric body is that it is conditioned
by thought, emotions and feelings, and this in turn affects
the physical form.

RADIANT FEELING-EMOTIONAL BODY

The feeling-emotional body represents a color flow of
desire energies which are based on memory and have to do
with creating a movement or energy flow of experiencing.
The soul determines the quality, a color flow of specific
vibrational energy frequencies, it needs for evolution. Each
particular color flow creates its own desire-energy which
consciously or unconsciously attracts the necessary environment for experiencing. Experiencing with the soul's
direction enables one to integrate the desired quality. The
individual's capacity to image manifests for creative action
through the feeling-emotional body; thus, the soul functions
through the feeling-emotional body to create desire-energies
and imagery for expansion.

RADIANT MENTAL BODY

The basic function of the mental body is to synthesize patterns of physical actions and feeling-emotional reactions with mental evaluation and discrimination in order to balance the three bodies. This is accomplished, after receiving inputs from the physical and feeling-emotional bodies, by utilizing active intelligence, discipline, memory, judgment and discrimination to evaluate and process the data. The mental body receives inputs from the soul for needed experiences which are put into action through the feeling-emotional and physical bodies.

An entity can be dominated by either the mental, feeling-emotional or physical body. Intense polarization in the mental body can lead an entity to separativeness by shutting out physical and feeling-emotional inputs. This can be repolarized by intuitional perceptions of soul awareness. Conversely, domination by the physical or feeling-emotional bodies necessitates the use of physical pain or feeling-emotional discomfort to activate the mental body to evaluate and process the data. The intensity of the experience, either feeling-emotional or physical, will determine the depth of evaluation. Thus, the mental body begins to function and a balance of the three bodies is initiated.

RADIANT BODY BALANCE

Preoccupation with any one aspect of life, at the exclusion of others, will result in an imbalance and seriously impede the process of expansion with conscious awareness. Figure 6 illustrates a feeling-emotional body that is out of balance in relation to the other radiant bodies. Such an imbalanced energy field may dramatically affect and influence the energy bodies around it. The same would be true of an imbalance in either of the other two bodies.

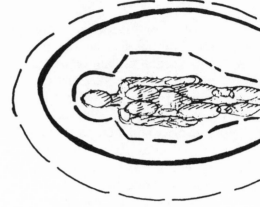

A COMPARISON OF BALANCED AND IMBALANCED RADIANT BODIES

BALANCED

IMBALANCED
(Emotional)

FIGURE 6

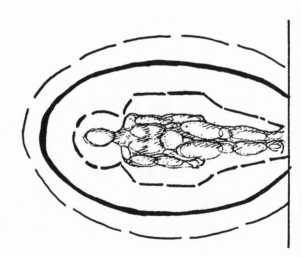

46

During a particular cycle of incarnation, a soul works through one (or more) of the three bodies of a personality which most closely corresponds to the needed quality. Soul and personality may express the needed quality more fully than other qualities to attain a greater balance with conscious awareness.

Balancing and integrating the radiant bodies is a prerequisite for achieving higher levels of conscious awareness. This course of study deals with the application of vibration, sound and color as an aid for integration. Vibration is frequency movement of energies which can create awareness through resistance to harmony. Sound has the capacity to penetrate all the radiant bodies and aid experiencing and flow. The use of a particular color assists in experiencing qualities it represents. Breathing is the rhythmic action which serves as a basis for energizing and communicating with all three radiant bodies.

Discussion 3:
Diaphragmatic Breathing

BREATHING AS A POINT
OF DEPARTURE

The natural breathing process for most individuals occurs as a normal event in daily life and is so biologically integrated that this life-giving function is generally an unconscious part of living. Little, if any, notice is taken of the component parts of the breathing process, such as breathing intervals, breath volume, or lung capacity. Only when this process is disturbed or distorted, do most individuals become aware or concerned. While the above breathing components are incidental to everyday life, they may require adjustments in order to develop a technique of diaphragmatic breathing. This technique becomes a means of departure into a greater state of self-conscious awareness and is referred to in this text as "esoteric breathing."

Ordinary breathing is not sufficiently attuned or rhythmic enough to induce an expansion in self-conscious awareness. Coordinating the physical, feeling-emotional and mental bodies requires specific effort and concentration. This entails learning new procedures, patterns and rhythms sufficiently different from the usual biological process to become a challenge. Esoteric breathing is an important and fundamental mechanism for producing harmonious soul sounds through the human form. The rhythmic aspect of esoteric breathing induces balance in the radiant bodies and is the initial recognizable state for meditation. Figures 7 and 8 depict stages of change once the effects of esoteric breathing are realized.

FIGURE 7

ESOTERIC BREATHING: STAGES OF CHANGE

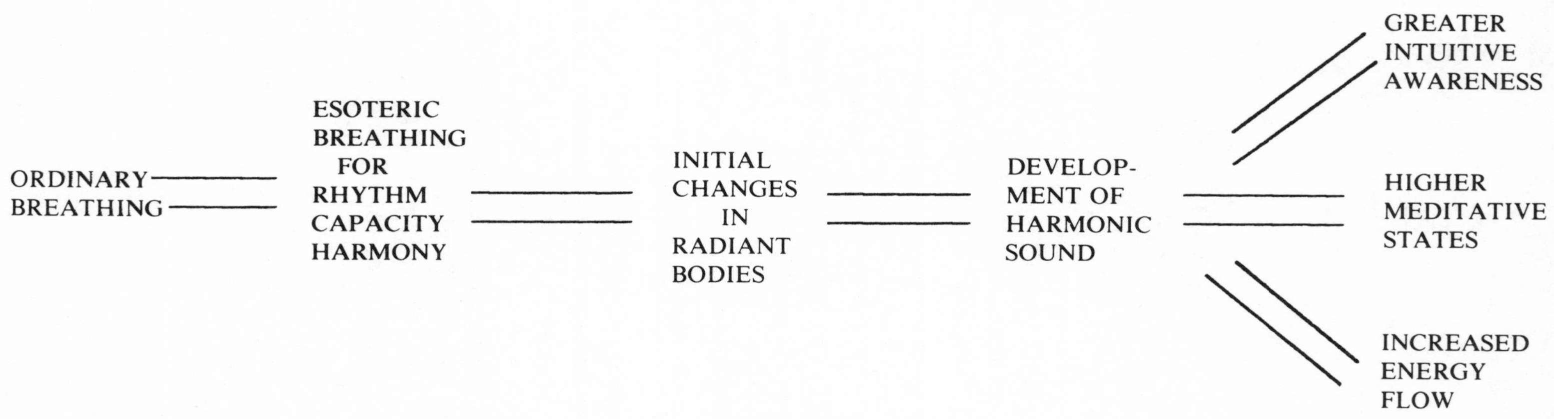

ORDINARY——
BREATHING——

ESOTERIC
BREATHING
FOR
RHYTHM
CAPACITY
HARMONY

INITIAL
CHANGES
IN
RADIANT
BODIES

DEVELOP-
MENT OF
HARMONIC
SOUND

GREATER
INTUITIVE
AWARENESS

HIGHER
MEDITATIVE
STATES

INCREASED
ENERGY
FLOW

ESOTERIC BREATHING AND RADIANT BODY BALANCE

FIGURE 8

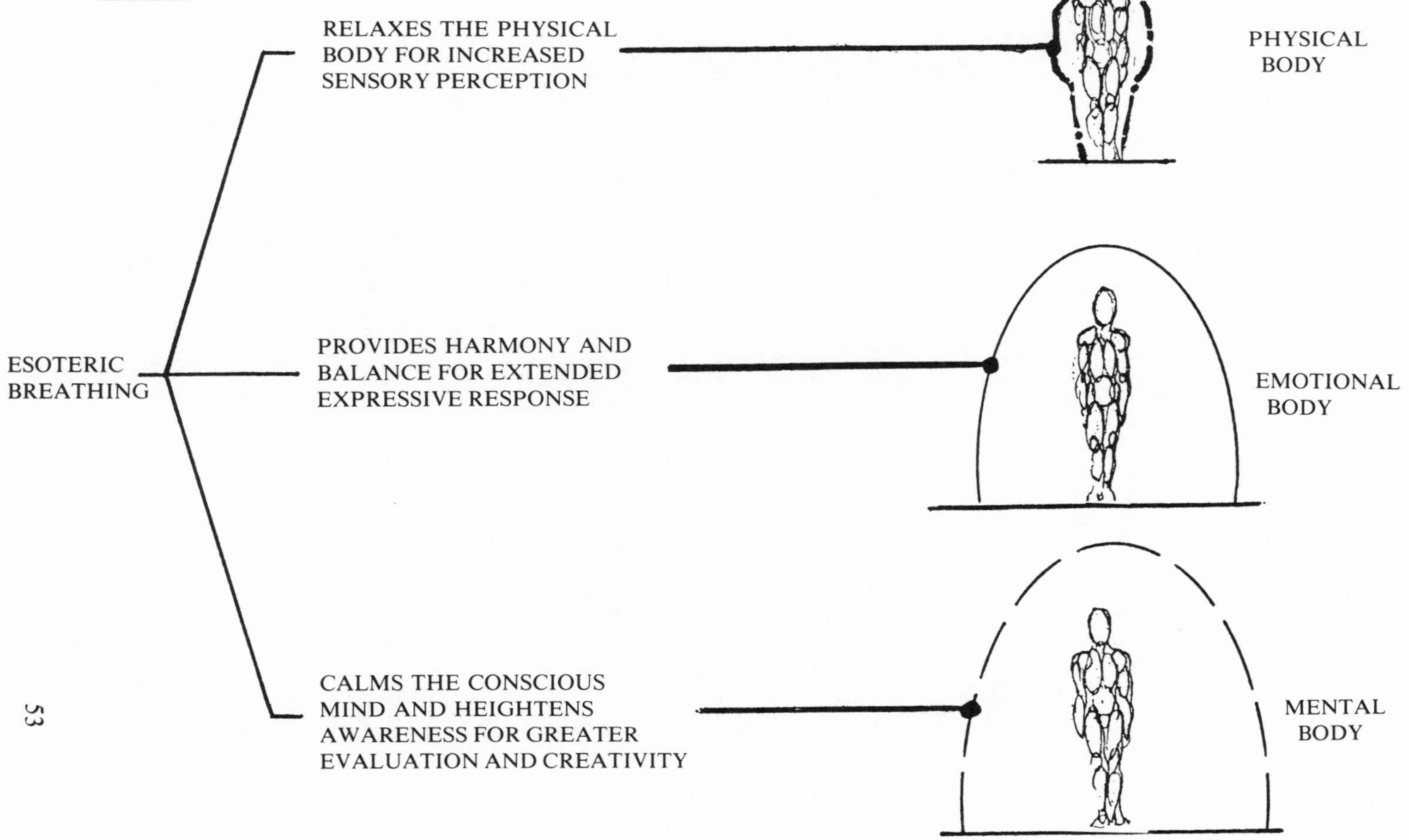

PHYSICAL BODY

EMOTIONAL BODY

MENTAL BODY

RELAXES THE PHYSICAL BODY FOR INCREASED SENSORY PERCEPTION

PROVIDES HARMONY AND BALANCE FOR EXTENDED EXPRESSIVE RESPONSE

CALMS THE CONSCIOUS MIND AND HEIGHTENS AWARENESS FOR GREATER EVALUATION AND CREATIVITY

ESOTERIC BREATHING

INHALATION-EXHALATION
TECHNIQUES
Eastern-Oriental and Western Esoteric
Breathing Schools

There are two basic inhalation-exhalation techniques, one originating with Eastern-Oriental cultures, and one with Western cultures. Inhalation-exhalation through the nose originated with yogic breathing exercises of the East and was designed to enhance the individual's conditioning for passive or internal states of awareness. Nasal breathing is considered conducive to introducing a contemplative state because air is inhaled and exhaled at a slower rate and will have a greater effect upon the head centers. The Oriental method is the same as the Eastern with the exception of the emphatic expulsion of breath through the mouth for action in the Oriental martial arts such as Kung Fu and Karate.

The Western technique uses open-mouth breathing which provides more air in a shorter period of time. This technique is conducive to an externalized state of activity and has a greater effect on the physical body below the neck. Nasal breathing has its primary effect on thought processes while open mouth breathing includes action with the physical form as well. Both techniques serve useful purposes and specific applications will be learned for each. Figure 9 illustrates both Eastern-Oriental and Western inhalation-exhalation techniques.

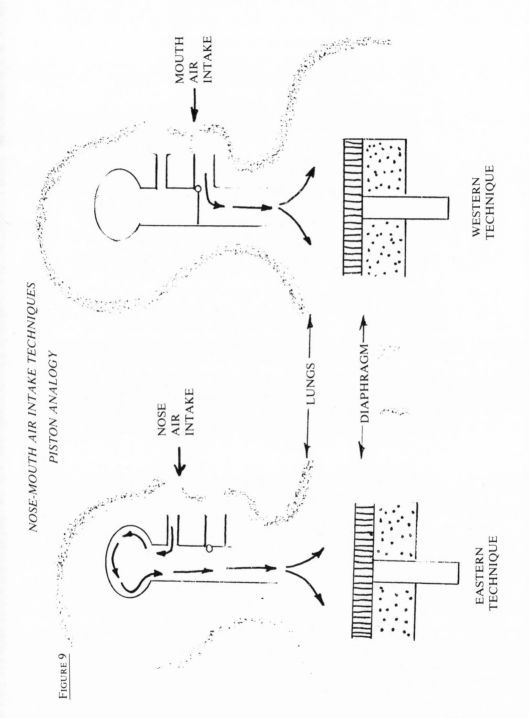

NOSE-MOUTH AIR INTAKE TECHNIQUES

PISTON ANALOGY

FIGURE 9

MOUTH
AIR
INTAKE

NOSE
AIR
INTAKE

LUNGS

DIAPHRAGM

WESTERN
TECHNIQUE

EASTERN
TECHNIQUE

55

THE ANATOMY OF
ESOTERIC BREATHING

Each individual will need to evaluate his usual breathing pattern. This assessment may reveal some surprising characteristics that are not compatible with esoteric diaphragmatic breathing such as rapid inhalation-exhalation intervals or shallow breaths using only the upper lungs; adjustment will be necessary through the diaphragmatic breathing techniques. Once a personal breathing assessment is made, the student may find that an adaptation in breathing technique requires improvement in physical conditioning. Body posture when sitting, standing or walking should be erect with the back straight, hips loose and shoulders relaxed to facilitate esoteric breathing.

The desired goal is to develop a diaphragmatic breathing technique which uses body mechanics not usually employed in routine breathing. The major difference is the use of the diaphragm as shown in Figure 10. Diaphragmatic breathing blends with routine breathing to enhance the vitality and capacity of the physical body.

The diaphragm is a thin muscle which separates the chest cavity from the abdominal cavity. It is located at the base of the rib cage. The triangular area between the rib cage and the abdomen is the *diaphragmatic area*. Proper diaphragmatic breathing causes this area to expand outward when the diaphragm is functioning at capacity as shown in Figure 10.

The following descriptions of esoteric diaphragmatic breathing techniques are used to simplify the student's understanding of the response of the physical body to an esoteric activity. We choose to use explanations we have found students understand easily instead of technical physiological terminology. Certain reactions such as hyperventilation or nausea may occur during the earlier stages of practice. A momentary pause to rest is advisable at this time. This is a manifestation of expansion taking place and should be no cause for concern. Moderation should be applied in the beginning, but perseverance will bring noticeable results.

The basic esoteric diaphragmatic breath consists of two steps: inhale and exhale. Assume a comfortable stance with the spine straight and the body relaxed. Fold the hands lightly over the diaphragmatic area to facilitate concentration and awareness. Take a deep breath through the mouth into the diaphragmatic area. You will feel the area expand outwards with your hands indicating the diaphragm is being utilized properly. As the diaphragm moves downward, the rib cage simultaneously moves upward and outward allowing the lower lungs more space to fill to capacity. As soon as you have completed the intake of air, exhalation begins by releasing the breath from the diaphragm upward through a relaxed throat and open mouth. The diaphragmatic area should contract at this point to its normal position if the breath was released properly.

Continue this inhalation-exhalation procedure in a regular in-out, in-out, 1-2, 1-2, rhythm. For balance and efficiency, use the same amount of time to exhale that was used to inhale. As you practice, you will become more proficient. Though subtle, energy abounds in each breath and provides generous amounts of vitality which may not be noticed until expertise is gained in using the new technique with awareness. *See Appendix, Exercise 1.*

Once the basic technique is well understood and can be executed with consistency, an additional *hold step* can be incorporated into the routine for specific creative purposes, such as producing esoteric sound, and for use in some of the exercises.

If needed, the *hold step* begins when inhalation is complete. The breath is retained by locking the rib cage open, keeping the diaphragmatic area fully expanded. Now energy can be dispensed to the radiant bodies through directed thought-forms, providing the additional vitality needed by certain areas of the body. Distribution of energy in this manner is very effective due to the heightened state of concentration at this time.

Once these basic steps are understood, sufficient practice is necessary to develop a natural frequency and rhythm. This is most important for attunement and expansion of consciousness. Although we stress learning the technique using the Western method of breathing, through the mouth, Eastern breathing through the nose can be adapted when deemed necessary.

Let us take a brief look now at the incorrect technique of diaphragmatic breathing caused by first expanding the upper chest on inhalation and then expelling the air by contracting the chest as shown in Figure 11. This is the method most used when instructed to "take in a deep breath and hold it." However, this technique of breathing is incomplete and inefficient for esoteric purposes.

CORRECT DIAPHRAGMATIC BREATHING

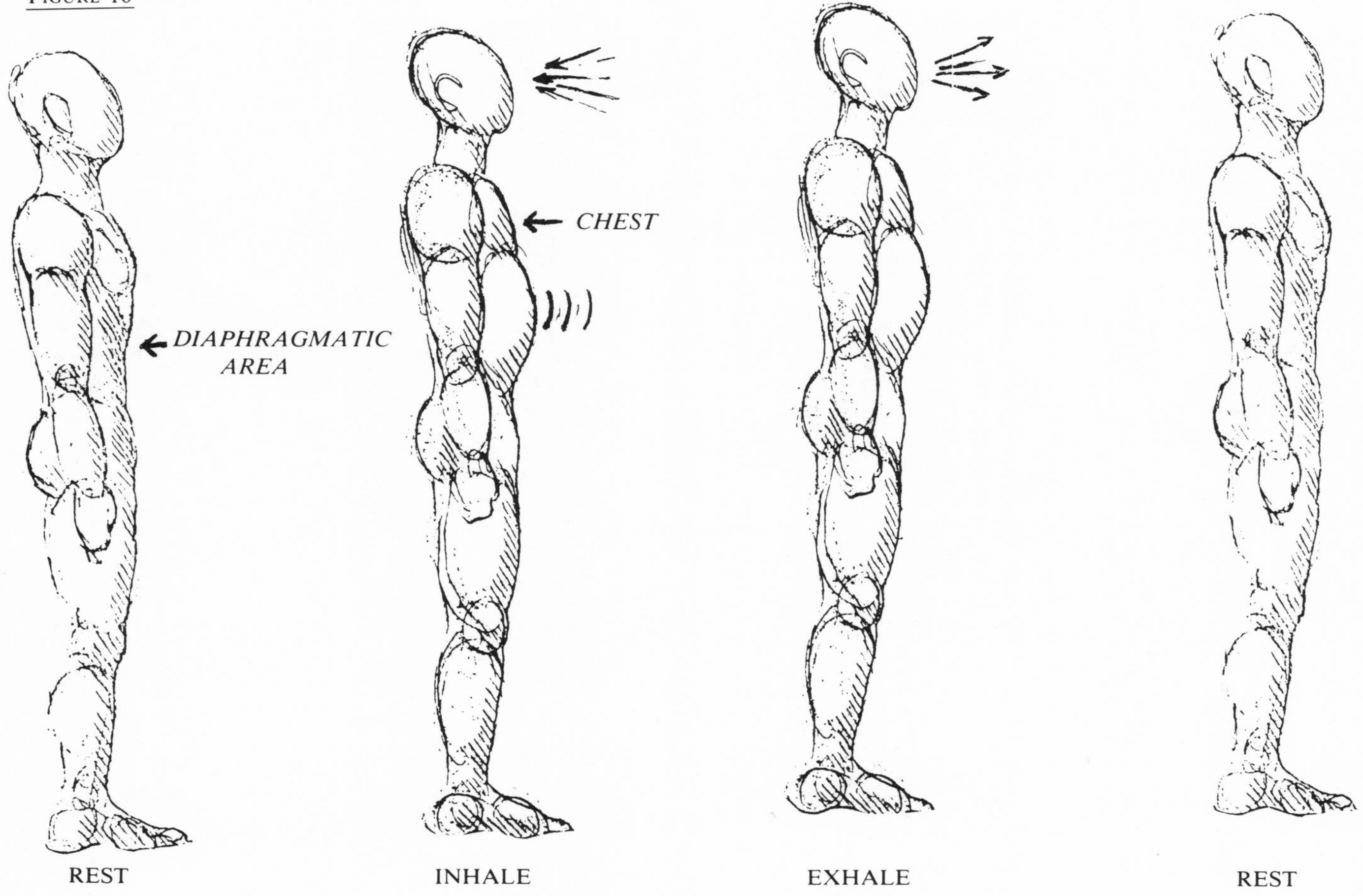

FIGURE 10

CHEST

DIAPHRAGMATIC AREA

REST

INHALE

EXHALE

REST

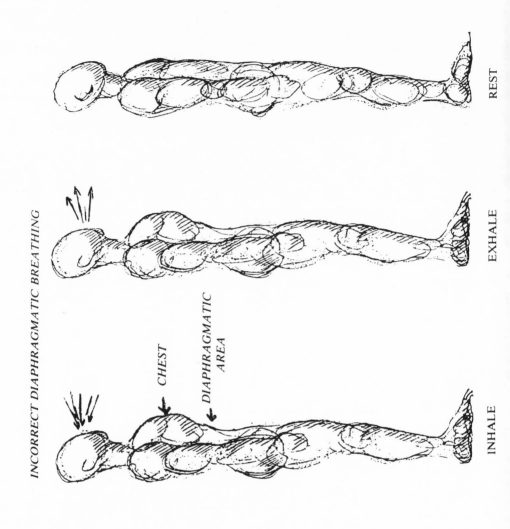

INCORRECT DIAPHRAGMATIC BREATHING

CHEST

DIAPHRAGMATIC
AREA

REST

EXHALE

INHALE

REST

Figure 11

60

Discussion 4: Sound

THE EFFECTS OF SOUND VIBRATIONS

This section deals with sound and its place in the evolutionary process of expanding one's conscious awareness. The discussion will be limited to the basic anatomy of sound and to principles of its application.

We are often unaware of the significance of sound in our daily lives. Constant bombardment from all sides by a seemingly endless number and variety of sounds is a part of our complex and increasingly technological civilization. Figure 12 illustrates how sound vibrations can impinge upon and distort the radiant bodies.

Sound is the manifestation and projection of the three-dimensional reality. It is a major contributing factor to the orientation and focus of our present state of conscious awareness. The principal difference between the undirected, random and distracting sounds of daily life and directed esoteric sound is that the latter produces synthesis and harmony instead of dissonance. Esoteric sound, employed in the presence of quiet solitude and thoughtful introspection, is a major factor in achieving higher levels of conscious awareness.

It is again recommended, when beginning to use these exercises, that the individual try to work with a group because the effect of this energy release brings change in the physical, feeling-emotional and mental awareness that may be disconcerting. Sharing these experiences within a group can provide needed objectivity and help achieve new understandings.

The vibratory effects of sound have definite physical manifestations. It has been demonstrated experimentally that different frequency sounds produce different geometric patterns or designs. The classic example of this is the geometric design produced by the sound of an instrument

63

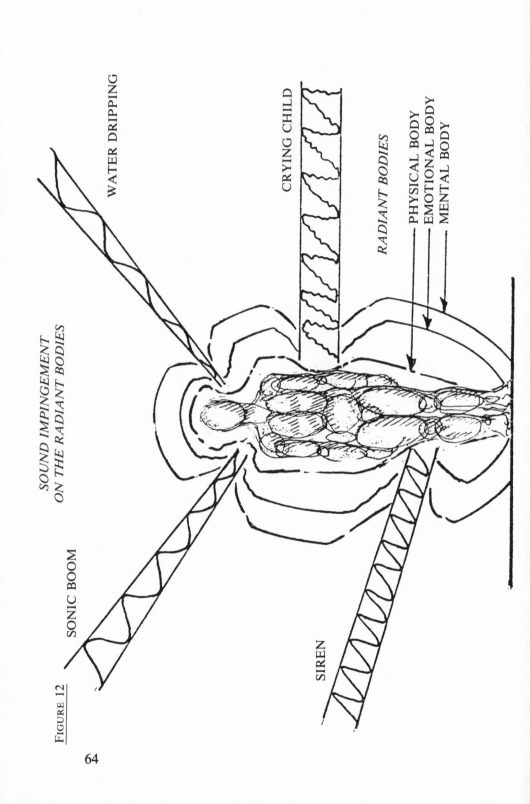

WATER DRIPPING

CRYING CHILD

RADIANT BODIES

PHYSICAL BODY
EMOTIONAL BODY
MENTAL BODY

*SOUND IMPINGEMENT
ON THE RADIANT BODIES*

SONIC BOOM

SIREN

FIGURE 12

64

playing in close proximity to a thin layer of sand on a surface like a drumhead. As the frequency of sound is varied,
the design varies. This quite vividly points out that vibratory
effects of sound can produce a definite rearrangement in
physical properties, though admittedly, this is an oversim-
plification of the effects of esoteric sound on the physical,
feeling-emotional and mental bodies.

When this principle is applied with esoteric sound, some
interesting manifestations result. For example, when one
learns to produce harmonious sound vibrations and men-
tally direct them inwardly toward the physical body centers,
a rearrangement for balancing and centering is acquired
which permits greater and more effective energy flow. Harmonious sound vibration directed with appropriate mental
thought disrupts negative qualities and transmutes them
into positive qualities. Esoteric sound vibrations shatter
rigid patterns in the radiant bodies. This can be noticeably
disruptive but necessary to bring about a centering of focus
and a new orientation.

Another example of the effects of sound is a law of
physics which states that when sound vibrations are projected on an object of the same natural frequency as the projected sound, the object will begin to vibrate in sympathy
with that sound. At this point, the object and the sound are
said to be in resonance. A simple, but rather profound,
analogy here is that if one may produce a sound which is on
the same natural frequency as the soul vibration, there will
be a transfer of soul energy. In fact, such a transfer does occur when individuals are able to produce their own personal
sound. The pitch of your speaking voice is your natural
sound frequency. However it should be noted that, for
most, efficient use of esoteric sound techniques comes
through persistent practice with conscious awareness and
living what needs to be experienced.

Two aspects of sound which can be produced by the
human voice are vowels and consonants. Vowels have more

open and harmonious characteristics than consonants and are more readily brought into resonance. Thus, esoteric sound utilizes the vowel sounds quite extensively. Table C gives the pronunciation and pitch of these sounds and their corresponding color qualities. Use the octave that is comfortable for you.

Vowel sounds are practiced for outer awareness and relating to others; consonant sounds are for inner awareness and development. The synthesizing sound which combines both outer and inner projections is the universal "OM" from the Tibetan schools. The "O" is for outer projection and "M" or "hum" for inner projection. Eastern schools, while utilizing this sound for centuries, have emphasized more the consonant sounds for inner awareness. Western schools combine the universal "OM" sound, the vowels, consonants and hum, into an integrated expression for both inner and outer awareness. The Oriental schools have emphasized both vowels and consonants for mental control of form.

TABLE C
VOWEL SOUNDS AND CORRESPONDING COLOR QUALITIES

SOUND	PRONUNCIATION	PITCH	COLOR
Ē	HE	C	RED
Ĕ	PET	G	ORANGE
Ä	AH	E	YELLOW
Ā	HAY	D	GREEN
Ō	OH	B	BLUE
Ü	WHO	F	PURPLE-VIOLET
ŌM	HOME	A	INDIGO

THE ANATOMY OF ESOTERIC SOUND

As with breathing, individual attention to one's normal sounds may reveal some interesting and surprising characteristics. Sound created by individuals is a reflection of their general state of Being and indicates quality aspects of their life. In general, higher pitch or faster frequency sounds indicate a mental orientation, while low sounds imply physical inclination. Nasal, broken or uneven sounds normally indicate a constriction in some particular center, usually the center for expression, the throat, or the feeling-emotional center, the solar plexus. Sounds which are off-pitch signify extreme imbalance in one of the radiant bodies and reflect a lack of conscious awareness and acceptance of one of the quality aspects of life.

Balanced radiant bodies and open physical body centers produce sound that has a magnetic resonant quality. These exercises may then be applied to correct or improve underlying conditions which influence the nature and magnetic quality of that sound. The following is a detailed discussion of methods and techniques for properly producing and directing esoteric sound.

The initial step in performing sound exercises should be a period of deep breathing to relax the physical body, energize and vitalize the body centers while stilling the conscious mind. At this time, enter into a quiet state of mental contemplation of what is to be accomplished through the use of sound. Figure 13 illustrates the recommended position for producing esoteric sound. The feet should be spread a little less than shoulder width apart, with the hands folded lightly over the diaphragmatic area for awareness of its movement. The head should be balanced and the mouth open, using the Western manner of breathing with the throat opened and relaxed—think of yawning. This provides a direct passageway for release of the sound.

67

FIGURE 13

RECOMMENDED POSITION FOR PRODUCING ESOTERIC SOUND

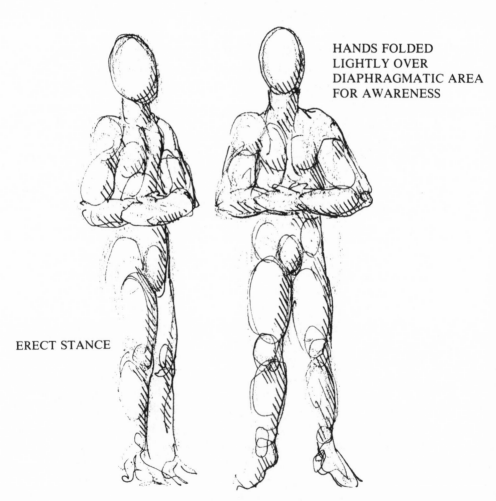

HANDS FOLDED
LIGHTLY OVER
DIAPHRAGMATIC AREA
FOR AWARENESS

ERECT STANCE

FEET SLIGHTLY APART

Now assume the proper position, exhale from the diaphragm to eliminate all air, then inhale deeply using the diaphragmatic technique learned in esoteric breathing. After deep inhalation, initiate the *hold step* by locking the rib cage open to keep the diaphragmatic area expanded and slowly make the sound, with the support of the diaphragm, as the breath is released up through a relaxed throat and mouth. The *hold* and *exhalation step* are used simultaneously for producing esoteric sound. You can provide controlled intensity and pitch to the sound from the diaphragm, without forcing or straining, by keeping the rib cage locked open.

It is important to remember that loudness or volume does not equate with the vibrational quality of sound. The mental body should be focused on the desired purpose and quality of the sound to be projected. As the breath subsides, the sound should also decrease in intensity until it terminates. The diaphragmatic area is expanded as long as the sound is being made. DO NOT PUSH THE DIAPHRAGMATIC AREA IN TO MAKE THE SOUND. If you can only make the sound for a short period with the diaphragmatic area expanded, stop the sound and inhale to again support the sound, or stop the sound and complete exhalation. With practice, your diaphragmatic area will expand sufficiently to allow maximum lung capacity for inhalation.

The vowel sounds of Ä and Ā are good to begin with to enhance consistency without any undue strain. The number of repetitions required to produce desired sound vibration will vary with each individual.

As with other areas of esoteric learning, the key to improvement and eventual success is discipline and practice. Establish a routine and adhere to it, selecting a period of the day that is convenient and a proper place for practice. It should be a time and area where a degree of solitude can be maintained and that is available for this purpose on a regular basis. By utilizing the same location, a vibrational vortex is built up over a period of time, producing a cumulative effect which allows each session to be started at a higher vibrational level. This eliminates the need for long periods of preliminary warm-up. It is also helpful to produce sounds in front of a mirror, observing one's stance, posture and breathing technique. A tape recorder is useful for evaluating your sound and progress.

FURTHER TECHNIQUE AND APPLICATION OF ESOTERIC SOUND

As one develops resonance and intensity while producing sounds, further attention can be directed to the qualities of those sounds. These qualities relate to the color associated with each vowel sound and are presented in Table A, Discussion 1.

A specific body posture is helpful in developing projective techniques of sound and color qualities. Figures 14–20 present the body posture and position for each of the seven vowel sounds along with its color and associated contemplative qualities while producing the sound.

Further, each sound has its own universal pitch and the serious student will work toward attaining that pitch. It should be accomplished without strain by starting at a lower level and gradually training the vocal cords to the desired pitch.

Application of the above techniques will begin to release to conscious awareness those qualities requiring additional experiencing and will also open the door to increased self-conscious awareness and altered states of consciousness. Use of these postures and sounds helps when working on the specific color qualities associated with each sound. While experiencing an emotion or quality associated with personal relationships in family, work or group, the use of sound and color with the associated posture enables the individual to flow with the experience of the emotion and quality, transmuting any resistance.

FIGURE 14

UNIVERSAL VOWEL SOUND Ē

PRONUNCIATION: Ē as in feet
COLOR: Red
PITCH: Middle C
QUALITIES TO CONTEMPLATE: freedom, will, power, strength, honor, determination, vitality, initiative and action
KEYNOTE: Will and Power

Stand erect with feet comfortably apart. Hang arms down from the shoulders with elbows bent, forearms extended and hands open. The arms are alternately thrust forward, then backward in short quick movements while making the sound of Ē vigorously.

FIGURE 15

UNIVERSAL VOWEL SOUND Ō

PRONUNCIATION: Ō as in oh
COLOR: Blue
PITCH: B above middle C
QUALITIES TO CONTEMPLATE: love-wisdom, kindness, gentleness, humility, trust, understanding, self-forgiveness, compassion, patience, cooperation and acceptance.
KEYNOTE: Love-Wisdom

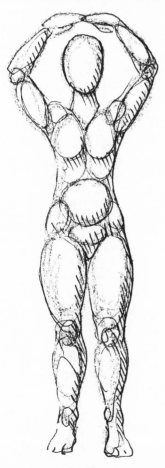 

Stand erect with feet comfortably apart; extend arms around head in an O shape, entwining the fingers to complete the circle and make the sound of Ō gently.

FIGURE 16

UNIVERSAL VOWEL SOUND Ä

PRONUNCIATION: Ä as in father
COLOR: Yellow
PITCH: E above middle C
QUALITIES TO CONTEMPLATE: joy, discipline, mental discrimination, evaluation, organization, justice, and harmony.
KEYNOTE: Active intelligence; joy of enlightenment; understanding

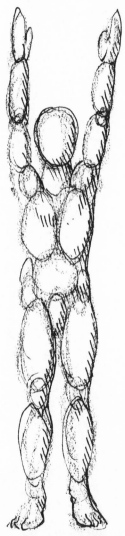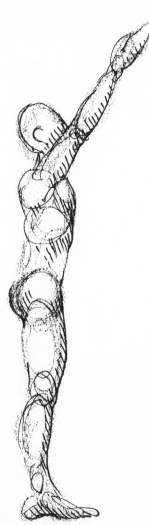

Stand erect with feet comfortably apart; extend arms upward and forward approximately 60° from horizontal. Face palms inward and make the sound of Ä joyously.

FIGURE 17

UNIVERSAL VOWEL SOUND Ā

PRONUNCIATION: Ā as in fate
COLOR: Green
PITCH: D above middle C
QUALITIES FOR CONTEMPLATION: all the qualities of blue and yellow plus growth, expansion, healing, hope, enthusiasm, gratitude and creative communication.
KEYNOTE: Resistance to harmony; brings expansion through experiencing.

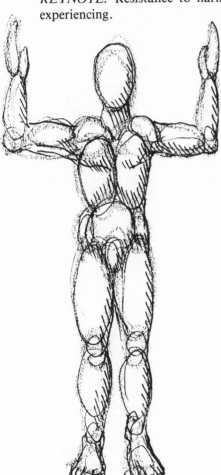 

Stand erect, feet comfortably apart; extend arms outward from the shoulders to form a cup with forearms bent upwards, palms facing inward. Make the sound of Ā with a sense of expansion.

FIGURE 18

UNIVERSAL VOWEL SOUND Ĕ

PRONUNCIATION: Ĕ as in let
COLOR: Orange
PITCH: G above middle C
QUALITIES TO CONTEMPLATE: all the qualities of red and yellow plus courage, change, confidence, illumination, steadfastness, inventiveness and intellect.
KEYNOTE: Materialization of thought into concrete form

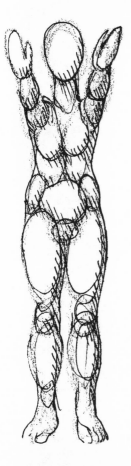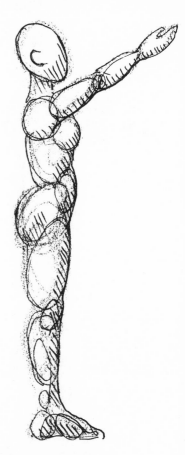

Stand erect, feet comfortably apart; extend arms forward and upward approximately 30° from horizontal with palms facing inward. Make the sound of Ĕ with a sense of confidence.

FIGURE 19

UNIVERSAL VOWEL SOUND U

PRONUNCIATION: Ü as in who or rue
COLOR: Purple-violet
PITCH: F above middle C
QUALITIES FOR CONTEMPLATION: all the qualities of red and blue plus devotion, release, idealism, loyalty and responsibility.
KEYNOTE: Devotion and responsibility

 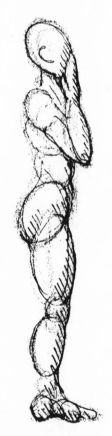

Stand erect, feet comfortably apart; make a cup of the hands by facing the palms outward, extending the thumbs at right angles to the fingers and touching the thumbs together. Place this cup under the chin and softly make the sound of Ü. This sound may be used very effectively for a sense of self-acceptance and release from guilt.

FIGURE 20

UNIVERSAL VOWEL SOUND OM

PRONUNCIATION: OM as in home
COLOR: Indigo
PITCH: A above middle C
QUALITIES FOR CONTEMPLATION: synthesis, unity, ritual, mastery and ceremonial magic.
KEYNOTE: Ceremonial ritual magic; invocation

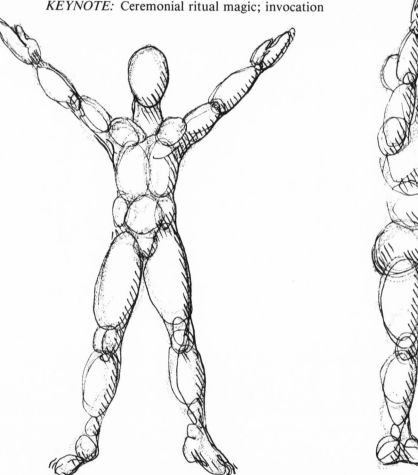

Stand erect, legs about 60° apart; extend arms upward and outward from shoulders about 60°. The body forms a five-pointed star with legs, arms and head as the points. Make the sound of OM in balance, sounding the O and M an equal amount of time and intensity with a sense of accomplishment.

Discussion 5: Color

ENERGY VIBRATIONS AND COLOR

Color awareness is usually more prevalent than awareness of sound and breathing. For most, this awareness stems from an interest in the aesthetic aspects of color more than from conscious recognition of a relationship between color and the basic qualities of life. During this discussion on esoteric color, such a relationship will be explored.

As a general introduction, it may be helpful to review some basic fundamentals of color and color manifestation. Figure 21 is a graphic representation of the electromagnetic spectrum. This spectrum consists of energy vibrations known as waves or rays which permeate throughout the known universe. These waves vary in length quite dramatically from one end of the spectrum to the other. At the cosmic end, wave lengths are so short that literally millions placed end to end will fit within an area the size of a postage stamp, while those at the opposite end of the spectrum may exceed one hundred thousand miles in length. To date, science knows very little about the extremes within this energy system.

Located near the middle of the spectrum is that very small band of radiant energy which is visible to man, the visible spectrum of light. As shown, this small band is divided into the basic colors that are perceived during daily life: red, orange, yellow, green, blue, indigo and violet. As with the total spectrum, the energy vibrations of each color within this band also vary in wave length.

Consciousness is dispersed throughout the Universe on rays of energy vibrations with each ray having its own vibrational rate and distinct set of life qualities. Each of us, as a soul-entity, has a point of origin in one of the primary color-rays, and our basic nature is reflected through the qualities of that particular ray. The intensity with which the soul is

81

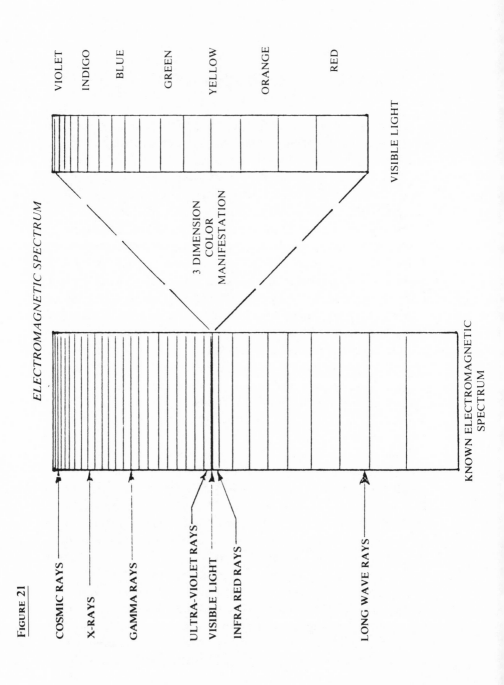

ELECTROMAGNETIC SPECTRUM

FIGURE 21

82

VIOLET

INDIGO

BLUE

GREEN

YELLOW

ORANGE

RED

VISIBLE LIGHT

3 DIMENSION
COLOR
MANIFESTATION

COSMIC RAYS

X-RAYS

GAMMA RAYS

ULTRA-VIOLET RAYS

VISIBLE LIGHT

INFRA RED RAYS

LONG WAVE RAYS

KNOWN ELECTROMAGNETIC
SPECTRUM

influenced by the ray of origin depends upon its point of evolution.

The electromagnetic spectrum is the medium, or at least one of the mediums, through which life qualities are transmitted. In our three-dimensional reality, that part of the spectrum which is visible to man, visible light, may be viewed as one of the mechanisms through which we experience these life or color-ray qualities. On other planes, or in other systems of reality, colors may be different or totally replaced by some other manifestations of expression.

Table A, Discussion 1, lists the seven rays, the color representing each ray, and qualities associated with each color. Through experiencing these various color qualities and their eventual synthesis, one achieves the balanced integration required for higher levels of conscious awareness.

As previously noted, our basic nature is reflected through one of the primary rays: red, yellow or blue. This is known as *the ray of the monad,* a primordial or archetypal force-field of energy. The soul is an extension of the experiencing monad. Since color is a vibrational manifestation of experienced qualities, the soul-entity's color emanation will be significantly changed according to the quality of experience during an incarnation. The personality or radiant bodies may need to experience through a different color-ray quality during a particular incarnation. Figure 22 illustrates this principle.

In *Letters on Occult Meditation,* Alice A. Bailey states that color is the form assumed by the life force as it moves, impeded or unimpeded, through a given material, its purity and clarity being determined by the vibrational rate (an expression of consciousness) of that material. This means that a soul-entity's color qualities reflect its point of evolutionary development and memory of various levels of conscious awareness.

A soul-entity's vibratory rate is continuously altered as

FIGURE 22

AN EXAMPLE OF ENTITY COLORS

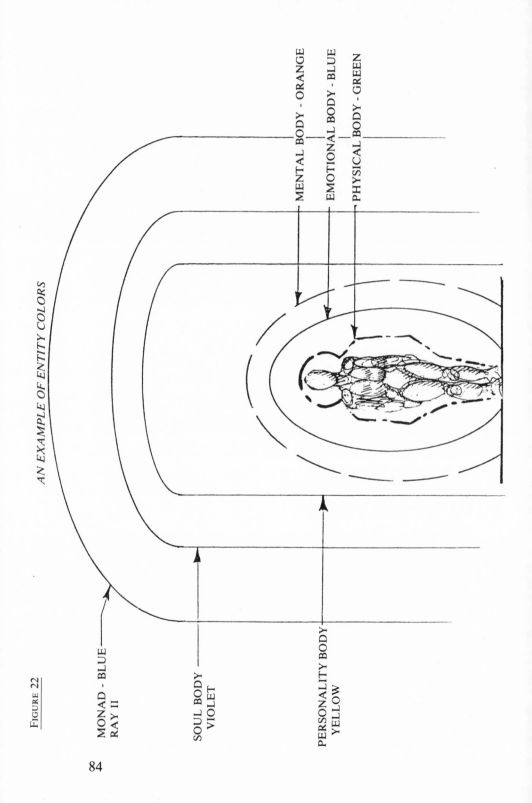

MENTAL BODY - ORANGE

EMOTIONAL BODY - BLUE

PHYSICAL BODY - GREEN

MONAD - BLUE
RAY II

SOUL BODY
VIOLET

PERSONALITY BODY
YELLOW

conscious awareness evolves, and these alterations appear as color changes in the auric field. As might be expected, color qualities of a mass conscious soul-entity are totally different from those of one who has achieved a degree of self-conscious awareness. This difference is reflected by the vibrational frequency of the two soul-entities; the former having a slow, sluggish rhythm with murky colors, and the latter having a pulsating movement with tremendous velocity and color clarity. As the radiant bodies become more refined by experiencing the life qualities, they are better conductive mediums for the expanding quality forces. A change in radiant body colors reflects this refinement.

For most students pursuing the path of esoteric knowledge, a wealth of experiencing has been achieved during previous incarnations. During some lifetimes, however, conscious awareness may be necessarily focused in the mundane physical aspects of daily life, preventing awareness of prior experiencing. As conscious awareness expands, a student's evaluating process is greatly enhanced and accelerated. Proper application and practice of esoteric color qualities will aid the expansion process.

EFFECTS OF ESOTERIC COLOR

The importance of color pertaining to human performance and behavior is a well-recognized fact. The commercial and industrial community acknowledges that work performance can be significantly enhanced through proper selection of color for office interiors, furnishings, etc. Medical facilities have based their color schemes on similar studies. Psychologists have for years used colors in the study of human behavior and therapeutic endeavors.

An evaluation of individual color tastes and habits may prove quite revealing. A consistent preference for the drab, murky colors in general, usually indicates self-doubt, worry, anxiety and a tendency toward criticism of self and others. An inability to match and coordinate colors, or to distinguish between primary colors, often denotes an imbalance and lack of sufficient experiencing or awareness of such experiencing. These characteristics can be corrected through experience and a new understanding of color. Significant progress may be made by surrounding one's self with brighter, more positive colors.

Self-evaluation should be made to become aware of one's individual responses, both positively and negatively, to the color qualities listed in Table D for self-conscious awareness. The determination and proper utilization of the specific color qualities needed will aid in correcting imbalance. For example, one who is timorous, lacking inner strength and courage, requires intensified experiencing of the color orange, which carries the vibration of courage and confidence. One lacking in self-acceptance requires further understanding of the qualities of blue.

Figure 23 illustrates a method for acquiring increased color awareness. This can be achieved by viewing a colored poster or a canvas, preferably painted by oneself, while concentrating on the quality aspects of that color. Reflected

86

color travels to the retina, the sensitive area at the back of the eye, which contains the color cones. Color in the cones is stimulated by continuous viewing of outside color, and the quality inherent in that color is transmitted to the medulla portion of the brain, or storehouse of prior experiencing.

Experiencing remembering increases the capability of perceiving color. After a period of concentrated practice, this process becomes automatic, and contact with various colors throughout the day will repeat the experiencing on a subconscious level and assist the memory process. Thus, qualities gained from prior experiencing are remembered and released to conscious awareness. This method is highly preferable to physically re-experiencing each of these qualities, and may be further enhanced with the addition of sound.

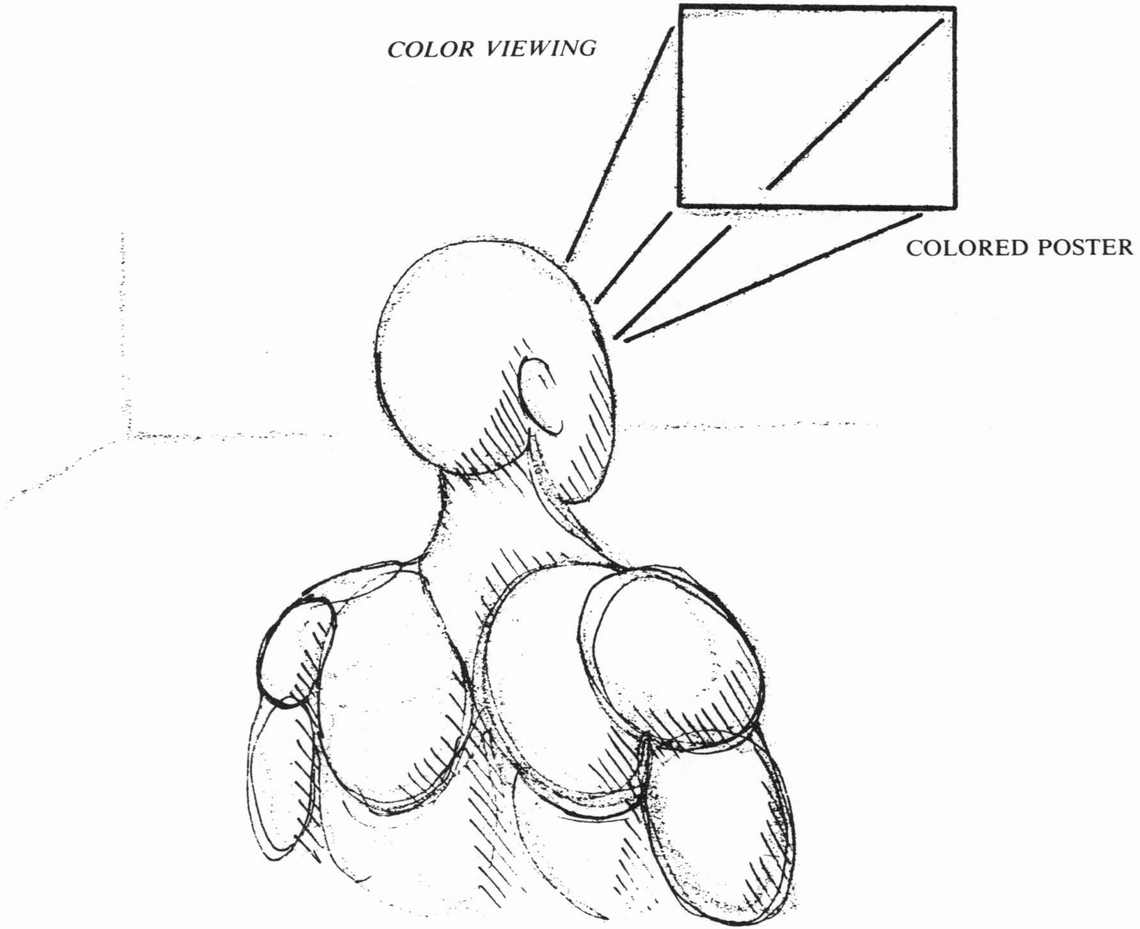

COLORED POSTER

COLOR VIEWING

FIGURE 23

88

VIEWING AURIC COLORS

Progress may be significantly enhanced through insight gained by viewing auric colors. Figure 24 demonstrates one technique for viewing these auric space colors. As shown, the line of sight is focused on the forehead and held for approximately 5-10 seconds, then quickly raised to a point above the head. The color seen will normally remain for only a brief period or until the line of sight becomes re-aligned and the cones of the retina override. The after-image first perceived is an initial state of the auric field. This process may also be used for viewing color around other areas of the physical form and is particularly effective above the shoulders. An individual's own color may be observed by performing this exercise before a mirror.

An excellent time for practicing this technique is during that period of the day which has been set aside for breathing, sound and meditation exercises. One should not become dicouraged by failure to see colors during initial attempts, as it normally takes periods of concentrated practice in any of these techniques to develop capability. Color or the lack of color around individuals depends upon their level of evolution. Individuals in early stages of evolution have not yet experienced sufficiently to radiate color, while those who are very highly experienced have become so light in their radiation that their color can be perceived only vibrationally.

It is interesting and quite gratifying to observe changes in one's own color as the body centers begin to open and the consciousness awakens. This experience is available to those who are willing to commit themselves to an organized program of study and practice.

There are many color techniques and systems of color viewing. Feel free to explore them and utilize the one that works most effectively for you at this point in time.

TECHNIQUE FOR VIEWING AURIC COLORS

FOCUS ON FOREHEAD
FOR 5 - 10 SECONDS

MAINTAIN HEAD STEADY
THEN ELEVATE THE GAZE
ABOVE THE FOREHEAD

REPEAT PROCEDURE
UNTIL AURIC COLORS
ARE READILY VISIBLE

NOTE: THE SAME PROCEDURE
IS USED FOR VIEWING
COLOR ABOVE THE
SHOULDERS

FIGURE 24

90

Discussion 6: Synthesis

Synthesis State
Integrative Processes Leading to
the Synthesis State
Table D

SYNTHESIS STATE

Synthesis is an evolved state which includes the combined effects of inherent capacities developed in past lifetimes and proficiencies being acquired now. As one becomes synthesized, potentials are enhanced and insights are acquired into more evolved states of consciousness. This is reflected by increased perception of vibration, sound and color in the three-dimensional Earth plane. Sound will be perceived as color; color will be perceived as sound. Levels of consciousness and their material manifestations are recognized, in their energy states, as unique vibratory forms which help to identify the evolutionary state. Synthesis is simply that state of consciousness where familiar and unfamiliar dimensions can be perceived, identified, analyzed and accepted with increased awareness.

Attaining the synthesis state can be aided by developing the basic esoteric disciplines of breathing, producing sound, and visualizing color. This process integrates potentials and proficiencies into a total vibratory Being. It also facilitates the progress of consciousness into a state of higher evolution as the individual becomes aware that the radiant bodies need balancing and maintaining.

Experiencing is necessary for resolution of incompleted actions and promotion of expansion. Enthusiastic participation in life is a requirement for achieving the synthesis state and for fulfilling the individual's portion of the greater plan. Each individual has a patterned development to experience for balancing incompleted actions. Within these confines and those of the greater plan, there is latitude in time and space.

Many individuals have developed a good background in esoteric disciplines through knowledge, but have been less determined in experiencing and living them on an everyday practical level. Difficulty in attaining a state of synthesis can usually be traced to an individual's resistance through fear, hatred, guilt, separativeness, lack of letting go, or complacency. These qualities prevent increased consciousness and obstruct the most vigorous attempts to expand.

Impediments of this kind take many subtle guises, such as insecurity, inconsistency, aloofness, apathy, or simply lack of motivation. No matter what disguise the hindrance takes, each individual must learn to recognize these resistances and impediments as major challenges which must be met, eventually experienced, and satisfactorily resolved. Avoidance or deferral will simply prolong the time required for complete evolvement.

Another hindrance to the attainment of a state of synthesis comes from cultural conditioning. Most world societies teach members, from childhood on, to maintain their attention and presence of mind within the confines of that culture's material and perceived world. It often requires extraordinary determination and motivation to overcome conditioning which focuses attention on the three-dimensional world and limits perception of other dimensions.

INTEGRATIVE PROCESSES LEADING TO
THE SYNTHESIS STATE

Evolution toward the synthesis state involves experiences which combine various qualities through the radiant bodies. These become integrative processes which create a whole that is greater than the sum of its parts. Integrative processes are seemingly simple in their most effective form; yet, they are intricately blended composites of fundamental traits. They provide stimuli to bring forth the inherent capacities for individual growth and expansion. Possession or absence of a needed trait is not always recognized until the task of self-expansion is undertaken. Once an individual initiates this task, a period of confusion and frustration often follows. A recognized goal or plan can provide necessary impetus, inspiration, and direction for continuing.

Integrative processes may be already developed in an individual and in various stages of being balanced, needing only refining through experience. And as they are manifested, they become more balanced or synthesized. Once developed, these processes aid in the balance and foundation needed for synthesis. There remains then the internalization process which occurs after practical application to verify competence of the newly integrated personality.

The following qualities are representative of the integrative processes:

AWARENESS: The level of awareness of an individual is reflected in his sensitivity to the physical world of color, heat and sound; the feeling-emotional world of love, fear and compassion; and the mental world of geometric patterns and designs.

Initially, one perceives with awareness physically, through the five senses: sight, smell, taste, hearing and touch. Reactions to these perceptions occur on a physical, feeling-emotional, and mental level. As sensitivity and

95

awareness increase, the five senses expand and more subtle ranges of qualities or vibrations are perceived through these five senses and through the sixth sense, called intuition. The increased capacity to react to these qualities brings a greater degree of detached involvement and wider range of response.

The ability to focus one's attention on subtleties of the newly acquired sensitivities enables one to gain greater awareness. Discipline of awareness is of singular importance in focusing one's attention. It will also provide vitality, feeling-emotional stability, and aid in creating a responsive spirit. This responsive spirit acts as a stimulus for enthusiasm, a major factor in generating interest and self-motivation.

SILENT SOUND: It is exceedingly difficult for modern man to maintain vocal and mental silence in the face of today's news media. The conscious mind is so filled with thoughts and details of the material world that an individual seldom finds time for private contemplation.

Contemplation is a state of creative meditation rather than a passive receptivity and does not require a trance or inactive mental processes as a prerequisite. The combination of active contemplation with the creative use of speech leads to constructive activity because words carry their own vibrations and those of the thought behind them.

EVALUATION: The process of evaluation is a response to changing internal as well as external stimuli. Internal stimuli are perceived through one's intuitive capacity and emanate from the soul's storehouse of completed and incompleted actions. The more one experiences and balances the incompleted actions, the more refined the evaluative capacity becomes. Through this process, one's point of view and system of values continually adjusts and realigns, further refining the evaluative process.

Each individual develops a particular process of evaluation and forms conclusions, without being judgmental, which enable him/her to extend calm persuasiveness based on creative thought and love. The ability to distinguish between subtle and more intense stimuli increases as self-conscious awareness increases. These stimuli are filtered through the individual's value system, assigned their relative importance, and a response is initiated. This is evaluation in action.

Objective evaluation develops the faculty of discrimination. Discrimination is the capacity to recognize, perceive and differentiate stimuli of the moment and determine the most appropriate reaction or response. This capability is a process which is constantly evolving and is a product of past experiencing and one's immediate cultural background of education, religion and geographical location. Experiential processes are constantly ongoing and add to the individual's wisdom by providing additional data for discrimination.

ACCEPTANCE: Acceptance is recognizing the necessity of experience; the process of letting go and letting be. Acceptance has no judgmental quality. It is simply to be aware. At times, experiences may be difficult and painful. Acceptance comes as they are recognized as stepping-stones for advancement to higher levels of awareness. Unlike inertia, resignation or passivity, acceptance is an active evaluation of existing circumstances and how these relate to the individual's life-plan, even if it requires the courage to initiate a necessary change in environment or consciousness. This process opens one for experiencing the flow of the soul's energy.

HARMLESSNESS: Harmlessness is love in action; a quality of gentleness and kindness that is non-diminishing to others. It is being inoffensive and unhurtful in action, word, and thought. Harmlessness is not produced or directed consciously, but is the "Beingness" of soul energy, experienced and accepted qualities. Practicing harmlessness requires a constant monitoring of one's reactions to external stimuli, knowing they are only a focus for an internal conflict that needs to be resolved. We invoke the soul energies needed from within to accept all that we are experiencing—such as anger, guilt, judgmentalness, criticism, etc.—through active contemplation, evaluation and release. This does not mean that we are to become passive, inactive, indifferent or totally self-restrictive. Rather, we are to be true to our own inherent goals and capacities and have a respectful regard for those of others.

The above five qualities serve as examples of the integrative process. Once initiated, these processes build on one another and the individual becomes the processes themselves, a state of synthesis.

Every individual has attained some levels of integration; however, few are willing to undertake the task of developing a greater sense of synthesis once the scope of the endeavor is understood. Mechanical attempts at achieving the synthesis state have a high drop-out rate because the spiritual as well as the physical realms must be involved.

The synthesis state develops slowly because of its complex nature. It is important to begin simply by incorporating diaphragmatic breathing into the daily routine. Perceiving color with renewed interest will awaken awareness of the qualities which each hue represents. If a certain quality-aspect of color is lacking in an individual, that depleted quality can be brought into balance by surrounding the environment with the color representing that quality. The use of color in a precise manner is not as important as the realization that the color itself contains vibratory qualities. Absorption of a color through the eyes, for instance, stimulates that color's qualities in the auric space.

Sound can be used similarly through awareness that each color is associated with a vocal and musical sound. Once the complementary vibratory effects of sound and color are understood, both techniques can be employed in developing a particular quality or achieving balance within the vibratory frequency of the quality.

Each individual is influenced by, and reflects, a dominant color ray. Identification of this ray and its sound-color qualities facilitates balancing within the radiant bodies. A chart correlating color and sound to various qualities is shown in Table A. Initially one should work with the sound-color most fitting immediate needs; later, the remaining sound-colors can be developed.

There is no prescribed method for acquiring the synthesis state. Individual needs must be considered and these can be complex. Table D illustrates basic elements of the integrative processes with corresponding color, sound, and exercises. Studying this chart with sincere introspection can lead to awareness of qualities that are most lacking or imbalanced.

For example, to balance the quality of over-sensitivity, one could choose to work with a pure blue color for detachment. This might include wearing blue clothing, viewing a blue canvas, listening to music which projects positive blue qualities, and becoming consciously aware of blue colors in the surrounding environment.

An additional aid in the process would be sounding "Ō" to the musical key of B. Regular practice of the recommended exercises will achieve the desired balance of the quality of sensitivity; however, the results will always be dependent upon the amount and consistency of time and energy invested in the process.

It is important to be aware of the general tendency to rush the developmental process; therefore, be prudent and moderate in the use of the techniques. Haste has the potential of turning one's efforts into mechanical achievement rather than authentic evolvement. The process should be allowed to evolve at its own pace through patient and consistent practice. Temperance and patience, through intuitive sensitivity and inherent wisdom, greatly assist achievement of the synthesis state.

TABLE D
INTEGRATIVE PROCESSES—TRAITS,
COLOR, BREATHING

	QUALITY TRAITS	COLOR	VERBAL SOUND	MUSICAL NOTE	BREATHING EXERCISES
AWARENESS	Sensitivity	Blue	Ō	B	# 1, 3, 8
	Attentive Focus	Yellow	Ä	E	# 2, 7
	Discipline	Yellow	Ä	E	# 5, 6, 7
	Enthusiasm	Red	Ē	D	# 4, 5, 12
	Responsiveness	Green	Ā	C	# 9, 11
	Self-Motivation	Red	Ē	F	# 1, 9
SILENT SOUND	Contemplation	Blue	Ō	B	# 1, 3, 9
	Effective Speech	Red	Ē	D	# 3, 6, 9
	Analysis	Orange	Ĕ	G	# 2, 6, 11
	Non-Judgmental	Blue	Ō	B	# 1, 3, 8
	Calm Persuasion	Indigo	ŌM	A	# 1, 3, 10
EVALUATION	Recognition	Yellow	Ä	E	# 2, 7, 8
	Perception	Green	Ā	C	# 5, 6, 7
	Differentiation	Yellow	Ä	E	# 2, 7, 8
	Realignment	Orange	Ĕ	G	# 6, 7, 12
ACCEPTANCE	Experience	Green	Ā	C	# 2, 5, 7
	Acknowledgment	Yellow	Ä	E	# 2, 7, 12
	Responsibility	Purple-Violet	Ü	D	# 5, 8
	Courage	Orange	Ĕ	G	# 3, 5, 11
	Letting	Indigo	ŌM	A	# 3, 4
HARMLESSNESS	Love	Blue	Ō	B	# 1, 10
	Gentleness	Purple-violet	Ü	F	# 1, 3
	Non-Diminishing Kindness	Green	Ā	C	# 2, 11
	Respect	Orange	Ĕ	G	# 3, 7, 12

SUMMARY

In conclusion, we hope that we have piqued your curiosity, expanded your perspective in some areas and motivated your desire to experience your soul's energies with conscious awareness. We encourage you to begin a program for expanded awareness, and experience the joy of transformation. There are no shortcuts, but with persistence and determination, these techniques will initiate many changes within your consciousness. The proper use of this system will facilitate an orderly progression of transformations and eliminate unnecessary chaos and confusion.

The changes will first take place in consciousness, and then begin to manifest in your outer experiences and relationships as you start to take responsibility for the creation of your own reality according to your soul's direction. We continue to urge you to work within the protection and stabilizing influence of a group which meets once a week for its members to practice, and share their experiences as they begin to be aware of the new and transforming energies of the soul.

Patience, persistence, determination, and sharing are the key qualities needed for reaping the rewards of this system. Remember, to grow we must experience the stress and strain of resistance to achieve the flow of harmony in consciousness. This is the expansion process through the green qualities of resistance to harmony; harmony to resistance.

Let not your hearts be troubled, for all soul-entities are moving toward expanded awareness within their own evolutionary levels as all begin to experience the energies of a new age.

Each one of us can start now to serve by increasing our own soul light to help enlighten and evolve all humanity, and our planet Earth, in an orderly progressive movement for efficiency. If readily met with awareness, the resistances need not be shattering—only challenges and opportunities to change and progress to a newer and better understanding of acceptance and Being.

This is the plan of the Hierarchy of Light Beings who believe change can now be effected without worldwide war or devastating natural catastrophe. It is our job to accept and cooperate; to be transformers of energies for growth and expansion as a great evolutionary step forward is taken. Old ways, traditions, and dogmas must be released to make way for a newer and greater perception of spiritual purpose as it is revealed. Ask and you shall receive; knock and it shall be opened to you. The Hierarchy is ready to instruct and aid all who seek to serve during this period. Are you ready?

Appendix

Exercises and Illustrations

INTRODUCTION TO THE EXERCISES

These exercises are designed to facilitate proper diaphragmatic breathing while promoting self-conscious awareness and the synthesis process. Practice them in sequence until you feel comfortable and then practice them as needed; but BE CAREFUL NOT TO DO MORE THAN 2 OR 3 OF THE EXERCISES IN ANY ONE DAY.

Exhale completely to clear the lungs of stale air before beginning any of the exercises. All exercises should be done to a slow, even count — such as the heartbeat. For balance, make the timing for exhaling the same as for inhaling. If hyperventilation or dizziness occurs, continue the exercise two more times to go beyond the point of resistance, for increased capacity; then rest for a while. The Western method of breathing will be used for these exercises except when other methods are specifically stated.

Exercise #1
Diaphragmatic Breathing

INHALE POSITION: Stand erect and place the hands on the relaxed diaphragmatic area. In the figure, the hands are shown at the side for clarity. Open the mouth and back of the throat as though yawning; start inhalation. Feel and hear the air moving through the mouth and throat. Continue inhaling until the diaphragmatic area is extended to its fullest as shown. Ordinarily, when we inhale, we think the diaphragmatic area goes in, but in esoteric breathing the diaphragmatic area expands outward on inhalation.

EXHALE POSITION: When the diaphragmatic area is stretched to its fullest, begin exhalation by pushing the diaphragmatic area in and releasing the air as if with a bellows. Feel and hear the air as it moves through the relaxed throat and open mouth. Continue exhalation from the diaphragmatic area until the lungs are emptied.

NOTE: Inhale and exhale at the same rate of speed, keeping the sound of the air moving through the throat evenly. Concentrate on moving the diaphragmatic area only, keeping the chest and abdomen as still as possible. Continue the breathing exercise five to ten times, or until slight hyperventilation or dizziness occurs.

PURPOSE: To take in prana for body energy; aid in gaining altered states of consciousness; release crystallized forms around the emotional center (the solar plexus, situated just above the diaphragmatic area); aid meditation, physical breathing, and mental counting.

EXERCISE #1: DIAPHRAGMATIC BREATHING

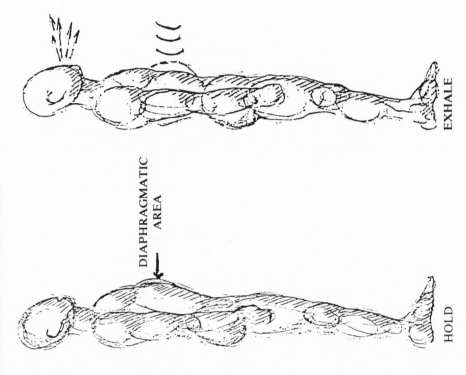

EXHALE

HOLD

DIAPHRAGMATIC AREA

INHALE

Exercise #2
Rhythmic Balanced Breathing

INHALE POSITION: Place the palms of the hands together in front of the body. Inhale using the diaphragmatic breathing technique learned in Exercise #1. As you inhale, slowly move the hands away from each other horizontally, stopping when the diaphragmatic area is extended to its capacity.

HOLD POSITION: When the diaphragmatic area is fully extended, the hands should be in a separated position as illustrated.

EXHALE POSITION: As you begin to exhale, the hands begin to move back together slowly. When the palms of the hands touch, the lungs should be empty.

NOTE: Time the inhalation and exhalation to the heartbeat. For example: four beats for complete inhalation, and four beats for complete exhalation. The hands serve as a measure of the air intake. When one's diaphragmatic area expands to a greater capacity, the hands should extend farther to the side. Strive to expand the diaphragmatic area and increase the air intake.

PURPOSE: To reduce hypertension and aid in developing a sense of peacefulness; to develop a measured, relaxed movement; to aid in becoming aware of one's vibrational frequency; to develop focused rhythmic patterns.

EXERCISE #2: RHYTHMIC BALANCED BREATHING

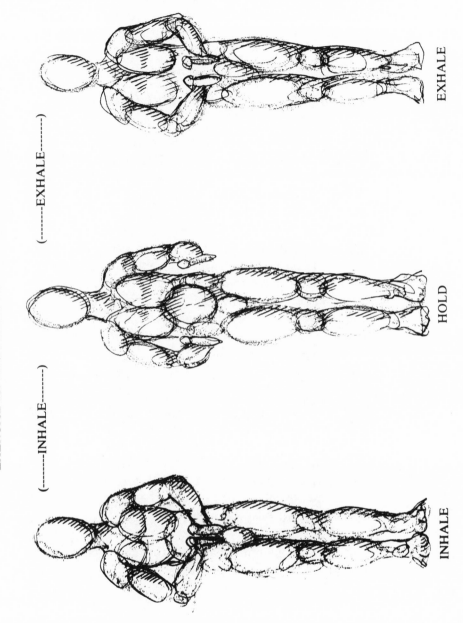

(------INHALE------)   (------EXHALE------)

INHALE   HOLD   EXHALE

Exercise #3
Diaphragmatic Control and Expansion

INHALE POSITION: Stand erect with your arms fully extended in front of your body as shown. Diaphragmatically inhale to capacity and hold by locking the rib cage and diaphragmatic area open.

HOLD POSITION: Close your mouth to keep the breath in and bend your trunk toward the floor, arms relaxed, as shown. Bend as far forward as comfortable. Anyone with back trouble should bend only as far as he feels is safe. While in the bent position, bounce the trunk up and down five times rhythmically.

EXHALE POSITION: After the fifth bounce, return to an upright position and diaphragmatically exhale.

NOTE: It is important to have the same sound and airflow rate for both inhaling and exhaling. Concentrate on balance and smoothness. The diaphragmatic area will expand as control is gained. Do this exercise one complete sequence two times a day. After the diaphragmatic area expands, you may increase the bounces in the bent-down position.

PURPOSE: To aid diaphragmatic control and increase diaphragm elasticity and capacity.

EXERCISE #3: DIAPHRAGMATIC CONTROL AND EXPANSION

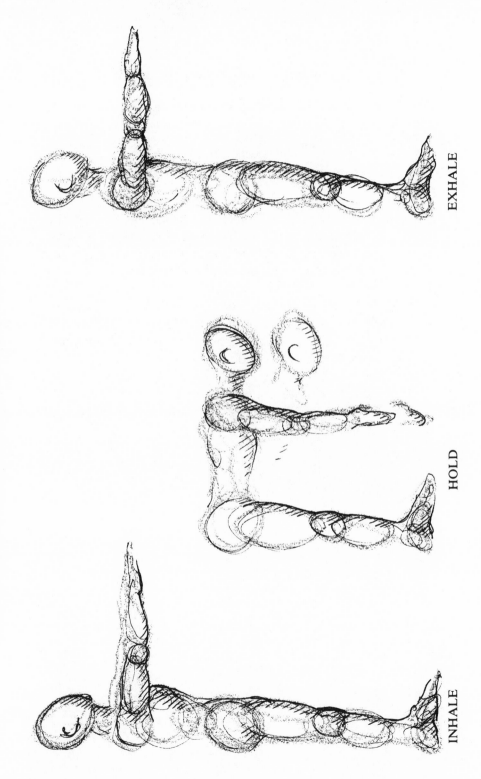

INHALE

HOLD

EXHALE

Exercise #4
Concentrated Diaphragmatic Control

INHALE POSITION: Stand erect and place hands over the diaphragmatic area to feel if the diaphragm is being used correctly. The diaphragm shows the arms at the sides for clarity. Inhale diaphragmatically.

EXHALE POSITION: Loudly and forcefully expel the air in short bursts with the sound of HUH! . . . HUH! . . . HUH! Push the diaphragmatic area out forcefully during each burst of sound.

PURPOSE: To develop force and volume for sound control; aid in releasing constrictions in the feeling-emotional center (solar plexus).

EXERCISE #4: CONCENTRATED DIAPHRAGMATIC CONTROL

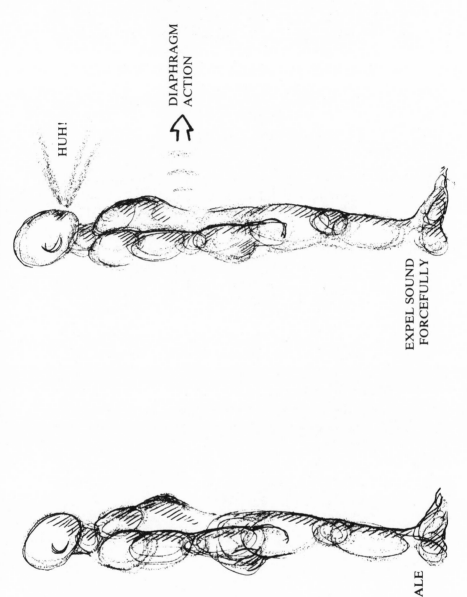

HUH!

DIAPHRAGM
ACTION

EXPEL SOUND
FORCEFULLY

INHALE

113

Exercise #5
Energy Breath

INHALE POSITION: Start the exercise in a standing posture, relaxed, but erect. Inhale diaphragmatically. Color can be added with inhalation for quality awareness.

HOLD POSITION: Hold the breath for three counts by locking the rib cage open with the diaphragmatic area expanded, not by tightening the throat. One count per heartbeat can be helpful.

EXHALE POSITION: Expel the air explosively in a loud SHH! . . . by forcing the diaphragmatic area inward.

NOTE: Repeat this exercise three to five times a day. Increase the length of holding the breath from three to six to nine counts until you are able to hold for one minute.

PURPOSE: To energize the body; to increase the power of concentration and control over the physical body.

EXERCISE #5: ENERGY BREATH

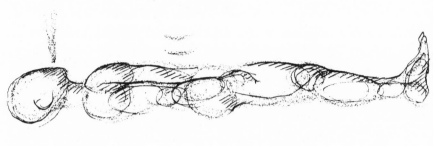

EXHALE POSITION
EXHALE EXPLOSIVELY
WITH A LOUD SHHHH!

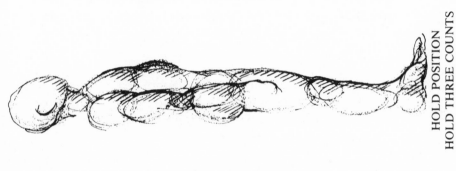

HOLD POSITION
HOLD THREE COUNTS

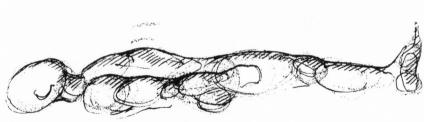

INHALE POSITION

Exercise #6
Butterfly Exercise

INHALE POSITION: Stand erect and relaxed. Inhale slowly, diaphragmatically, while rotating the arms in complete circles forward like the swimmer's butterfly stroke during the complete inhalation.

HOLD POSITION: Hold the breath diaphragmatically with mouth closed and throat open for ten heartbeats, keeping the arms outstretched to the side, parallel to the floor.

EXHALE POSITION: Exhale *slowly,* diaphragmatically, while simultaneously lowering the arms to the sides. Strive to finish expelling the air at the same time the arms reach the sides of the body.

NOTE: Do only two a day to start. Increase the number of exercises slowly according to your capacity to complete them without hyperventilation.

PURPOSE: Develops breath control; helps concentration and aids in developing patience.

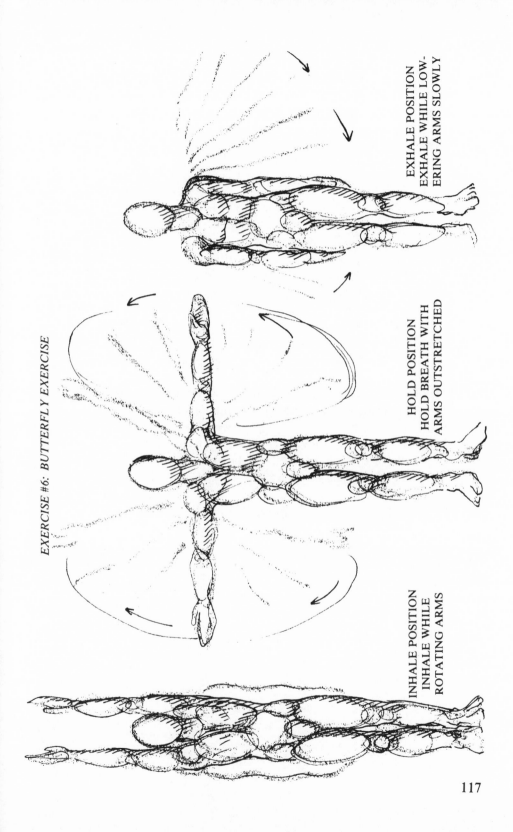

EXERCISE #6: BUTTERFLY EXERCISE

EXHALE POSITION
EXHALE WHILE LOW-
ERING ARMS SLOWLY

HOLD POSITION
HOLD BREATH WITH
ARMS OUTSTRETCHED

INHALE POSITION
INHALE WHILE
ROTATING ARMS

117

Exercise #7
Whirlygig Exercise

INHALE POSITION: Stand erect, legs comfortably apart, arms outstretched to the sides and parallel to the floor. Inhale diaphragmatically, rotating the *upper torso* back and forth in a circular movement. Flex the knees slightly but do not move them. Continue the rotation until a full breath is taken.

HOLD POSITION: Hold the breath diaphragmatically for a count of ten heartbeats, keeping the arms outstretched.

EXHALE POSITION: Exhale diaphragmatically while rotating the arms and torso as in the inhalation step.

NOTE: Do two of these exercises once a day, increasing the length of time in the hold position according to your breath capacity.

PURPOSE: Makes the diaphragm more flexible; expands the lung capacity; increases concentration.

EXERCISE #7: WHIRLIGIG EXERCISE

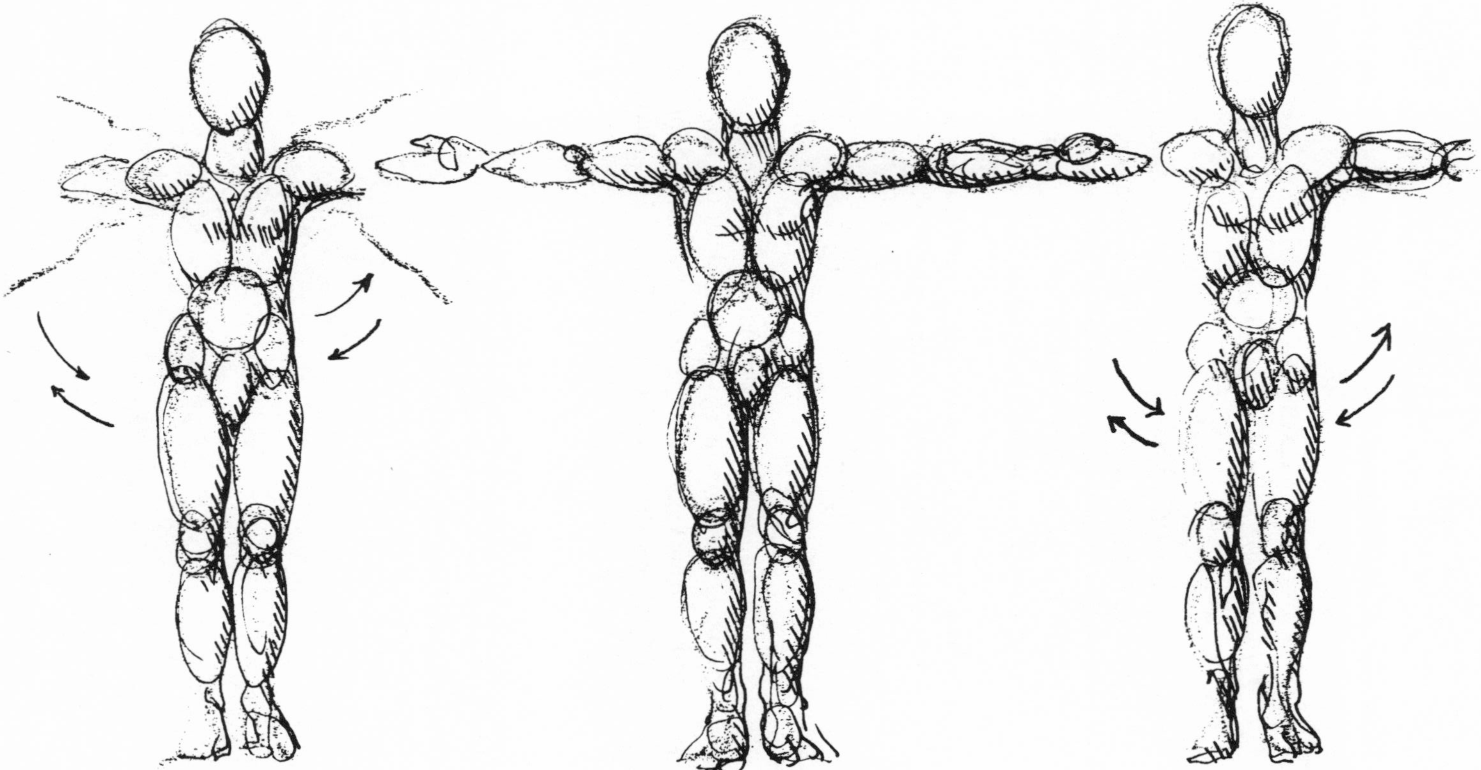

INHALE STEP
ROTATE UPPER TORSO

HOLDING STEP
HOLD 10 COUNTS

EXHALE STEP
ROTATE UPPER TORSO

119

Exercise #8
Discrimination Development Breathing

INHALE-EXHALE POSITION: Stand or sit erect and relaxed. Breathe diaphragmatically, using the Eastern method through the nostrils. Begin to inhale-exhale in quick tempo with short deep breaths. Inhale-exhale as many times as you can comfortably to complete the exercise.

NOTE: Imagine drawing the breath up between the eyes; bathe the discrimination area with air. The nostrils and bridge of the nose may feel cool during this exercise, which is an indication that the process is operating effectively.

PURPOSE: Expands the discrimination center for greater awareness and sensitivity to be able to identify odors and fragrances. This helps in relating to the vibrational energies of others or environmentally. It is also an aid in altering conscious awareness.

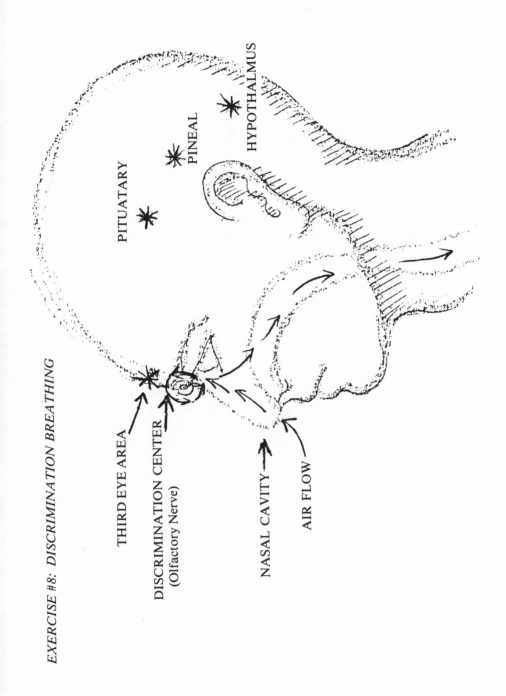

EXERCISE #8: DISCRIMINATION BREATHING

THIRD EYE AREA

DISCRIMINATION CENTER
(Olfactory Nerve)

NASAL CAVITY

AIR FLOW

PITUATARY

PINEAL

HYPOTHALMUS

Exercise #9
Receiving and Giving

INHALE POSITION: Stand erect, arms fully outstretched in front with palms up. Inhale, diaphragmatically, through the nose in the Eastern manner for eight staccato breaths, bringing the hands toward the chest a bit more with each breath and count. At the end of the eighth count, the palms should be touching the chest and the diaphragmatic area fully expanded.

HOLD POSITION: Hold the breath, diaphragmatically, for eight heartbeat counts. Hands should remain on the chest.

EXHALE POSITION: Exhale, diaphragmatically, through the mouth for eight short staccato breaths as you make the sound of SHH! Slowly extend the arms, palms up, to an outstretched position with each count. This is the reverse of the inhale step. At the end of the eighth count, you should be in the starting position with the breath expended and arms fully outstretched.

NOTE: Gradually increase this exercise to three or four times, once a day.

PURPOSE: To increase coordination between the mental and physical bodies; to increase energy; to expand receptivity and giving faculties.

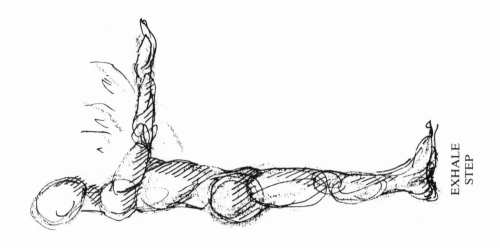

EXHALE
STEP

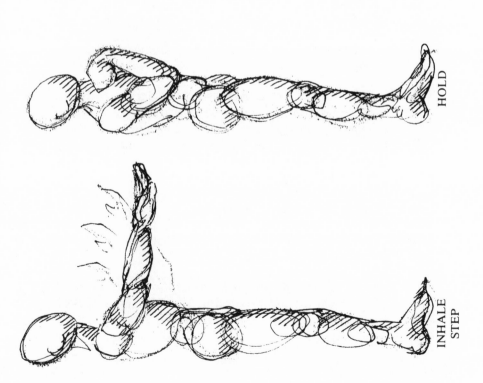

HOLD

INHALE
STEP

Exercise #10
Head Rolls

INHALE POSITION A: Stand erect; inhale, diaphragmatically, through the nose in the Eastern method.

HOLD POSITION A: Completely relax neck and shoulders. Roll head slowly in three complete circles clockwise (right to left). Re-center the head erect; rotate the head slowly toward the right; slowly back to center; slowly toward the left; slowly back to center.

EXHALE POSITION A: Exhale breath slowly through the mouth with a low SHH! . . . until all air is expended.

INHALE POSITION B: Inhale fully, diaphragmatically, through the nose.

HOLD POSITION B: Remain relaxed; roll the head slowly three times counter clockwise (left to right); re-center the head; rotate the head slowly toward the left; slowly back to center; slowly toward the right; slowly back to center.

EXHALE POSITION B: Exhale slowly with a low SHH! . . . until all the breath is expended.

NOTE: Repeat up to four complete cycles at first. Strive for a longer holding period.

PURPOSE: Develops a sense of being consciously centered with relaxation and expansion; a greater sense of flexibility and balance; releases the throat center for fuller expression.

EXERCISE #10: HEAD ROLL

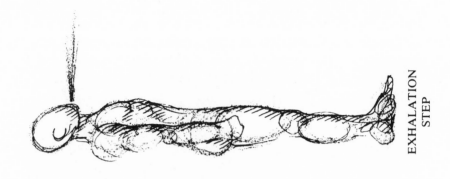

EXHALATION
STEP

HEAD TURN
STEP

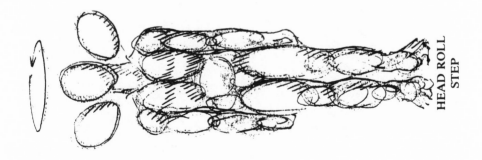

HEAD ROLL
STEP

Exercise #11
Walking Exercise

INHALE POSITION: Stand erect; start walking briskly forward, left foot first. Take eight steps, inhale a short breath diaphragmatically with each step. Eight short inhalations should equal one full breath.

HOLD POSITION: Hold the breath diaphragmatically and about-face, military fashion, with a pivot.

EXHALE POSITION: Walk back briskly to the starting point, left foot first. Exhale eight short breaths diaphragmatically with each step. Upon completion of the eighth step, all air should be completely expelled. About-face and repeat the exercise.

NOTE: Do this exercise two times, once a day. Gradually increase to five times, once a day. This exercise can be done when walking normally, omitting the about-face.

PURPOSE: To develop confidence and posture for rhythmic effect of movement. To develop concentration and control of the form.

EXERCISE #11: WALKING EXERCISE

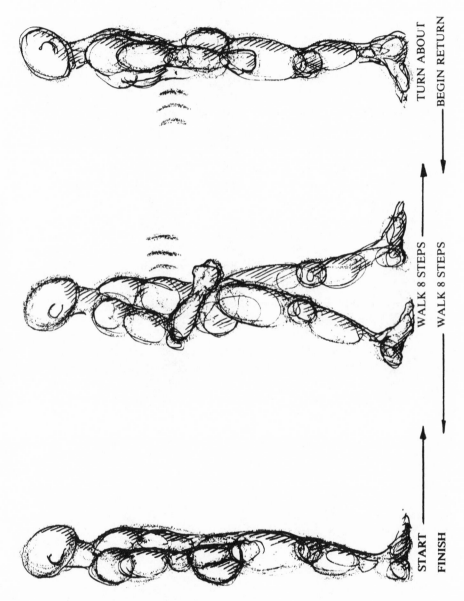

START ——————— WALK 8 STEPS ——— WALK 8 STEPS ——— TURN ABOUT
FINISH   BEGIN RETURN

Exercise #12
Kundalini Flow Alignment Exercise

INHALE POSITION: Stand erect with arms outstretched in front of the waist and palms touching. Bend slightly forward at the waist and flex the knees a little. Inhale diaphragmatically as you move your arms outward in a sweeping motion to the side until fully extended at shoulder height.

HOLD POSITION: No hold position.

EXHALE POSITION: Exhale diaphragmatically as you return the body and arms to the starting position in the same sweeping movement, except bring the arms up beyond the waist to head height and stand erect.

NOTE: Repeat three times, once a day. You may inhale color for greater flow of restricted or depleted qualities.

PURPOSE: To bring any blockage in the kundalini into flow.

EXERCISE #12: FLOW ALIGNMENT EXERCISE

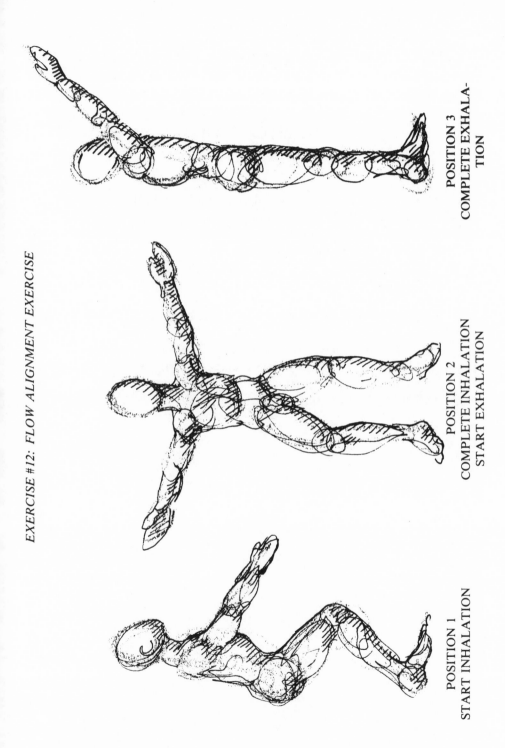

POSITION 3
COMPLETE EXHALA-
TION

POSITION 2
COMPLETE INHALATION
START EXHALATION

POSITION 1
START INHALATION

Exercise #13
The Hum

INHALE POSITION: Sit or stand erect and inhale diaphragmatically through the mouth or nose.

HOLD-EXHALE POSITION: Begin to generate the *hum* sound . . . "Hum-m-m-m-m." In making the sound, you are using the breath, which is like exhaling.

NOTE: Do it daily as many times as you can.

PURPOSE: To bring a flow movement between the radiant bodies, releasing any crystallized patterns within the bodies; for self-protection against any outer forces intruding within your psychic space.

GLOSSARY

Acceptance—to understand the energy frequency of the life quality that has been experienced, without feeling guilt, regret, remorse, excessive pride, possessiveness, or separativeness.

Christ—the completed soul consciousness of Earth's experiences. Each planet has its completion of all that is within that vibrational frequency at that point in evolution.

Consciousness—awareness of Being, I AM.

Crystallization—a restriction in consciousness caused by the repetition of learning and experiencing without acceptance of change and expansion in consciousness from the experience.

Desire—the feeling-emotional nature of the soul which motivates the experiencing needed to become a creative Sun.

Disciple—the beginning consciousness of responsibility to self when awareness goes through certain extremes to bring the desire qualities under control through the discipline of patterns for future unfoldment into the Christ consciousness.

Duality—the individualization of energy into consciousness by experiencing the masculine electric (+) energies and feminine magnetic (-) energies of Earth's thought-forms.

Energy Frequencies—vibrational rhythms; the essence of the composition of all light which constitutes consciousness and form.

Enlightenment—wisdom (See Wisdom)

Evil—constriction, wanting to retard the process of expansion against universal law.

131

Feminine—receptivity, gentleness, kindness, compassion, grace, peace, reflection, cooperation, passivity, acceptance, dependence, vulnerability.

Good—the willingness to experience and live life as creatively as possible with acceptance.

Hierarchy—those Beings who have achieved cosmic consciousness and operate from a level of soul awareness. They serve as a group to plan and direct the expansion process in the solar system while continuing their own evolutionary process.

Illusion—a guide from level to level for experiencing one's ideas and ideals; but if one does not accept the experiencing he may be said to be "illusioned."

Innocence—inexperienced but willing to accept the process.

Intuition—the faculty of direct knowing through feeling sensitivity to soul wisdom. Only a mature soul manifests this capability with awareness.

Karma—a cycling process for the soul to experience all of Earth's qualities as cause and effect creating a balanced awareness.

Kundalini—the portion of soul energy which extends into the form and unifies the consciousness of the physical, feeling-emotional, and mental bodies. This soul energy is both experienced and yet to be experienced energy which begins then to pulsate a unified field of energy that creates genius awareness.

Love—an active conscious awareness of acceptance of the experiencing process to self and others.

Masculine—will, power, action, force, strength, courage, confidence, freedom, independence, and leadership.

Master—the initiate who accepts with serenity the oneness of purpose behind duality and becomes Christed in consciousness.

Non-Acceptance—unwillingness to accept life's lessons as they are given and the disillusionment it often entails;becoming cynical, bitter or vindictive.

Qualities of Life—the experiencing with awareness of vibrational thoughtforms or ideas and desires as seen in the seven color rays. (Table A)

Reincarnation—process of a soul force-field through cycles of many lifetimes of experiencing all the life qualities to become Christed.

Rhythm—vibrational frequencies of an energy quality of life. Numbers are symbolic representations of these energy frequency progressions.

Self-Conscious Awareness—the awareness of being an individualized soul that has memory and the evaluative capacity of the experiencing process.

Spirit—the essence of the energies of the Solar Logos or God to be experienced and understood by the soul.

Soul—that portion of spirit energy that proceeds to experience in the solar system to gain individualization of consciousness as a co-creative point of light.

Soul-Entity—a given personality in incarnation through which the soul is experiencing as it evolves.

Universal Awareness—the realization of the unity of "all" through diversity.

Universal Law—cycles and patterns of energies that follow a certain magnetic movement from a center (sun solar system) that sets up the cycles for experiencing.

Universal Mind—that collective consciousness of all that has been experienced which is available to those with intuitive capabilities.

Universal Plan—the plan that all cell souls of light are in the process of expansion through resistance to harmony by experiencing darkness into light becoming co-creative Suns.

Wisdom—experienced knowledge; acceptance of the lessons of life.

If you have enjoyed this book, you will benefit from a set of two casette tapes (100 minutes), *Meditation with Colors, Sounds and Songs,* prepared by William David. The tapes contain the beautiful vowel sounds representing the seven rays, as well as one mantra and two songs for each ray. The purpose of the presentation is to aid you in developing your own sound proficiency while facilitating an awareness of energy relationships. Listening to and repeating the vowel sounds, mantras, and songs helps to cultivate the consciousness of joy and acceptance.

For information on how to obtain this set of tapes, please send a stamped, self-addressed envelope to:

Meditation Tape
The Sedona Research Foundation Inc.
4741 E Paradise Lane
Phoenix, AZ 85032